W9-BNU-691

THE NEW
NEW ENGLAND
Cookbook

THE NEW
NEW ENGLAND
Cookbook

125 RECIPES THAT CELEBRATE THE RUSTIC FLAVORS
OF THE NORTHEAST

STACY COGSWELL

WITH TAISSA REBROFF

PAGE STREET
PUBLISHING CO.

PAGE STREET
PUBLISHING CO.

First published in 2015 by

Page Street Publishing Co.

27 Congress Street, Suite 103

Salem, MA 01970

www.pagestreetpublishing.com

Distributed by Macmillan, sales in Canada by The Canadian Manda Group.

18   17   16   15   1   2   3   4   5

ISBN-13: 978-1-62414-177-5

ISBN-10: 1-62414-177-3

Library of Congress Control Number: 2015938778

Cover and book design by Page Street Publishing Co.

Photography by Jennifer Blume

Printed and bound in USA

Page Street is proud to be a member of 1% for the Planet. Members donate 1 percent of their sales to one or more of the over 1,500 environmental and sustainability charities across the globe who participate in this program.

THIS BOOK IS DEDICATED TO

my grandmother, Carmen Bouchard and my uncle, Ronald Bouchard who are no longer with us. Both taught me from a young age how to cook. I might not be in the profession I am in if I did not spend the time I did in the kitchen with them. I love you and miss you everyday.

Contents

WINTER

MENU #1

Pork Belly with Braised Pine Nuts and Roasted Quince — 67-68

Fresh Pasta with Bolognese Sauce — 71

Lobster and Celery Root Bisque — 72

Arugula Salad with Almonds, Green Olives and Blood Orange — 75

Braised Pork Shanks with Spinach Dumplings and Garlic Chips — 76-79

White Chocolate Pound Cake with Candied Grapefruit and Grapefruit Caramel — 80-83

MENU #2

Tomato Bisque with Fresh Mozzarella and Basil — 84

Endive Salad with Grapefruit, Roasted Pistachios, Roasted Beets and Pistachio Pesto — 87-90

Clams and "Spaghetti" with Spicy Garlic Croutons — 93

Spicy Chicken Stew with Cornmeal Dumplings — 94

Braised Short Ribs with Parsnip Puree and Squash Slaw — 97-98

Chocolate Mint Bread Pudding — 101

SPRING

MENU #1

Crab Cakes with Bacon Emulsion and Jicama — 105-107

Red Leaf Lettuce with Asparagus, Rhubarb and Lemon Poppy Vinaigrette — 108-111

Seared Scallops with Orange Braised Baby Carrots, Sweet Pea Puree and Pea Tendrils — 112-116

Rack of Lamb with Olive Oil Crushed Potatoes and Minted Fava Beans — 119-120

Vanilla Custard with Poached Rhubarb and Fresh Strawberries — 123-124

MENU #2

Sweet Pea Soup with Fresh English Peas and Parmesan Custard — 127-128

"Buffalo" Fiddleheads with Gorgonzola, Bibb Lettuce Cups and Buffalo Sauce — 131

Boston Lettuce Salad with Pickled Red Onions, Smoked Salmon Bacon
and Green Goddess Dressing — 132-137

Bucatini with Nettle Pesto and Pancetta — 138

Pan-Seared Chicken with Mustard Lemon Spaetzel and Roasted Beets — 141-142

Roasted Apricots with Yogurt, Honey and Almond Brittle — 145-146

SUMMER

MENU #1

MENU #2

STOCKS

FOREWORD

No one has ever accused New England of being edgy, especially in its cuisine. Yet in the past decade, Boston has become a gastronomical force, attracting—*and producing*—some of the best talent this industry has seen north of the Big Apple. As a Brooklyn native who started out in New York City kitchens, I can say it wasn't until I settled here (first in Rhode Island, then Massachusetts) that my own culinary voice found its broadest range.

In *The New New England Cookbook*, Stacy Cogswell combines an innate love of her native New England with an unbridled passion for cooking and a work ethic that is refreshing, if not rare. At the tender age of 34, this young up-and-coming chef is already making waves *and* news, as much for her charisma as her cooking. When I first met Stacy, she was aglow with the attention resulting from her appearance on Bravo's *Top Chef*. But instead of letting it go to her head, she was squarely focused on answering the question "What's my next move and how do I get there?" As I listened, and as we went back and forth about food, family, personal life and career, I realized she reminded me of myself at that age and, well, I wanted in.

I became a fan and champion of Stacy Cogswell that afternoon. Today, I am proud to share a kitchen with her at Liquid Art House in Boston. Just like her food, there is nothing pretentious about her. Stacy represents that hometown girl who works hard and tells it like it is. And, although she naturally identifies with New England cuisine, it is her relentless experimentation and work experiences in some of the greatest kitchens of our time that allow her to tell her this unique culinary story.

From the heart of New England, Stacy Cogswell cooks just for you, straight from the heart.

—Rachel Klein, Executive Chef, Liquid Art House

INTRODUCTION

This book is essentially my love letter to New England. All of the recipes found throughout these pages celebrate the wonderful ingredients and traditions found in the region. These recipes embrace traditional New England fare, but with a twist. They certainly aren't your grandma's recipes, but you'll love and crave them just the same. New England is a beautiful land and a great place to cook. All four seasons are experienced and the produce is abundant, providing plenty of inspiration throughout the year.

I decided to organize this book as a series of seasonal menus for a couple of reasons. As a professional chef, I always find it easier to envision a recipe within the scope of a menu, rather than as a stand-alone item. Yet having various menus to choose from gives you the freedom to make the entire multiple-course meal or just one dish from it. You can even mix and match dishes from different menus. It's really up to you!

I do, however, encourage you to stay true to the seasons. Cooking seasonally is very important to me, not only because the produce that's in season yields the most flavor, but also because it enables you to make the most of local farmers' markets. These menus are designed to celebrate the seasonal bounty in the New England area, so if a particular ingredient doesn't look good where you live, feel free to use what does. Don't get hung up on finding the listed ingredients if they aren't ripe; simply use what is fresh and appealing to you instead. I encourage you to experiment with these recipes. Use them as a guide, but don't be afraid to improvise. There is no such thing as kitchen mistakes, only happy accidents that sometimes turn out to be memorable dishes (see Braised Pine Nuts on page 68).

Above all, don't ever take yourself too seriously—cooking isn't a science, even if baking is. Have fun in your kitchen! And remember, a happy cook makes happy food.

Stacy Cogswell

Fall

Fall is a beautiful time in New England—the leaves begin to change color, the mornings are crisp and the excitement of the holidays is right around the corner. It's a cozy season and the food is rightfully hearty and warm. This chapter explores all the flavors of fall and offers menus that bring to mind apple picking, pumpkin carving, warm cider and the smell of fresh fallen leaves.

These recipes, as most good dishes should, celebrate the bounty of the season. The predominant flavors in this chapter are based on the ingredients found in New England during the fall months, like apples, pumpkins, root vegetables, squashes, cranberries and end-of-season corn. These are naturally at their peak during this time, but if they're not available where you live or if you're using this menu off-season, then I recommend you rework the recipe and use the fruit or vegetable that's in its prime.

Fall is also the time to embrace fat! We're talking about butter, duck fat, cream and all that good stuff. Soon we'll be bundling up for winter so it only makes sense to prepare ourselves appropriately. I love braising, roasting and *confit-ing* when the weather gets cooler, and that's what you'll find in these recipes.

Happy fall, and stay cozy!

PUMPKIN BISQUE WITH ROASTED GARLIC MARSHMALLOWS AND SPICED PEPITAS

I can't imagine a more fall-appropriate dish than this soup. It incorporates everything I love about this season into one bowl: pumpkin, spice and marshmallows. The savory marshmallows are an impressive touch, elevating this dish from just regular soup to a potential dinner-party course. The bisque is silky and tastes like fall and the marshmallows just melt in your mouth, while the pepitas add a nice crunch to each bite.

This recipe calls for fresh pumpkin for a reason. Canned pumpkin can sometimes have an artificial taste when used in savory dishes, so please take the time to prepare the real deal.

YIELD: 8 TO 10 SERVINGS

PUMPKIN BISQUE

1 (4 lb [1.8 kg]) pumpkin

2 ½ lbs (1 kg) bacon, chopped

2 ½ lbs (1 kg) onions, sliced

1 lb (455 g) leeks, sliced

2 cups (480 ml) sherry

2 tsp (5 g) nutmeg

1 tbsp (7 g) Chinese five spice

5 sage leaves

2 tsp (5 g) chili flakes

2 tbsp (30 g) salt

4 quarts (3.8 l) Vegetable Stock (page 197)

Roasted Garlic Marshmallows (page 18)

1–2 tbsp (8–16 g) Spiced Pepitas (page 21)

1 tsp (5 g) sea salt

Preheat the oven to 400°F (205°C).

Cut the pumpkin in half and scrape out the seeds. Roast the pumpkin cut-side-down until tender, about 1 hour. Once cool enough to handle, scrape out the flesh and throw the skin away. Set pumpkin aside.

Render the bacon in a stockpot for 15 minutes. Add the onions, leeks, sherry and spices and cook for 15 minutes, until tender. Add the roasted pumpkin and vegetable stock. Cover and let simmer for 15 minutes.

Puree the soup in a blender. If making ahead, allow the soup to cool and store in an airtight container in the refrigerator for up to 4 days.

Pour the hot bisque into your serving bowl and drop in the marshmallows. I like to use a kitchen torch to brûlée the top of the marshmallows. Sprinkle the pepitas and sea salt on top. Serve right away.

ROASTED GARLIC MARSHMALLOWS

This recipe can seem extremely intimidating and weird, but I promise you two things: it's actually pretty simple once you get the hang of it and savory marshmallows are a delicious, unexpected complement to a dish. The sweet, roasted garlic flavor pairs quite well with the Pumpkin Bisque (page 17).

Although the garlic can be omitted in this recipe to make the traditional, sweet 'mallows you know and love, I think that you'll start craving marshmallows in a whole new way after trying these.

YIELD: 10 TO 15 SERVINGS

MARSHMALLOW SYRUP

1 cup (240 ml) water

2 ⅔ cups (510 g) granulated sugar

½ tsp cream of tartar

½ tsp salt

ROASTED GARLIC PUREE

2 cups (300 g) garlic cloves

2 cups (475 ml) canola oil

MARSHMALLOWS

¼ cup + 1 tbsp (75 ml) cold water

2 gelatin packets or 1 ½ tsp (6 g) gelatin

⅓ cup (80 ml) water

¾ cup (180 ml) Marshmallow Syrup

2 tsp (10 g) salt

1 tsp pepper

¾ cup (145 g) granulated sugar

1 cup (240 ml) Roasted Garlic Puree

For the Marshmallow Syrup, place all of the ingredients into a 4-quart (4-l) heavy pan and bring to a boil over medium-high heat. Insert a candy thermometer into the pan, and boil, without stirring, until the syrup reaches 140°F (60°C). Remove the syrup from the heat and let it cool for 15 minutes.

For the Roasted Garlic Puree, place the garlic and canola oil into a small saucepan and cook over low heat until the garlic browns and is soft, about 15 minutes. Remove from heat and let cool to room temperature.

Once the garlic and oil have cooled, strain the oil and set it aside—I like to save mine for other cooking projects. Puree the garlic in a blender or, if you don't have a blender, you can place the garlic in a bowl and crush it using the back of a spoon until it forms a paste.

To make the Marshmallows, place the cold water and gelatin into the bowl of a KitchenAid® mixer. Set aside to allow the gelatin to bloom.

In a saucepan, bring the rest of the ingredients, except the garlic puree, to a boil. Cook until the temperature reaches 280°F (138°C). Remove from the heat and set aside.

Turn on the mixer and start breaking up the bloomed gelatin on low speed, then slowly drizzle in all of the sugar mixture. Once all of the sugar mixture is in the bowl, cover with a towel and turn the speed up to high. Whip for 10 to 15 minutes, until light and fluffy. Add the garlic puree in batches on medium speed.

Spray a half sheet pan with pan spray and cover it with plastic wrap. Spray the plastic wrap with the pan spray. Pour the marshmallow mixture onto the plastic wrap and level it out using a spatula. Cover it and refrigerate for 24 hours.

After 24 hours, you can cut the marshmallows into ½-inch (13-mm)-size pieces. If not using right away, you can store them covered in a refrigerator for up to a month.

SPICED PEPITAS

Although these Spiced Pepitas are the perfect little crunch your Pumpkin Bisque (page 17) needs and wants, they can also be used to garnish salads. The Cajun seasoning makes them salty, spicy and very addictive.

YIELD: 1 CUP (160 G)

1 cup (160 g) pepitas

2 tbsp (30 ml) canola oil

2 tsp (10 g) salt

2 tsp (10 g) pepper

1 ½ tsp (4 g) Cajun seasoning;
I recommend McCormick brand

Preheat the oven to 350°F (177°C).

Mix all ingredients in a bowl. Transfer to a sheet pan lined with parchment paper and bake in the preheated oven until toasted and slightly dark, about 10 minutes.

FRISÉE SALAD WITH CONFIT APPLES, CHEDDAR, CANDIED PECANS AND MEAD VINAIGRETTE

This crisp autumn salad manages to be hearty without overwhelming the meal, and it's also great simply served on its own as a light dinner. It's the perfect marriage of fall flavors—the sweetness of the apples and pecans is offset by the salty cheddar and acidic vinaigrette.

YIELD: 2 SERVINGS

1 head frisée lettuce

4 oz (120 g) chunk of aged cheddar

4 cups (800 g) Confit Apples (page 25)

½ cup (50 g) Candied Pecans (page 26)

¼ cup (59 ml) Mead Vinaigrette (page 27)

Prepare the frisée by cutting off the bottom and rinsing under cold water. Set aside to dry.

Using a vegetable peeler, peel the cheddar into thin shards.

Gently toss the frisée, cheddar, Confit Apple, pecans and vinaigrette until combined. Serve immediately.

CONFIT APPLES

This recipe is a delicious solution to the plethora of apples you get from apple picking in the fall, and it just so happens that it's pretty versatile, too. Gently cooking the apples for a long time gives their sugars a more savory flavor. In addition, the woodiness of the vanilla and the rich, slightly bitter olive oil help offset the apples' sweetness.

Confit Apples are great on all types of salads, but they also work quite well as an accompaniment for pork and chicken dishes.

YIELD: 12 SERVINGS

6 Fuji apples

2 cups (473 ml) olive oil

2 cups (473 ml) canola oil

1 vanilla bean, split

1 cinnamon stick

3 allspice peppercorns

3 bay leaves

3 rosemary sprigs

Cut all apples in half and remove their cores, then cut into quarters.

Add all ingredients to a large saucepan and slowly bring to a light simmer over medium heat. Cover with parchment paper so the apples cook evenly. Cook for 5 to 10 minutes until the apples are slightly tender. Remove the pot from the heat and allow the apples to steep in the hot oil until fully cooled, about 20 minutes.

Note

If kept in oil in the refrigerator, Confit Apples will last for up to a week.

CANDIED PECANS

These sweet and spicy pecans are an easy way to add an extra little somethin' to any salad. I like them in the Frisée Salad (page 22), but they're so tasty that you can make them work in many ways. They're also an irresistible snack—it's hard not to munch on them as they sit on your countertop!

YIELD: 2 CUPS (240 G)

2 cups (240 g) pecans
2 cups (383 g) sugar
2 cups (473 ml) water
1 tbsp (15 g) salt
2 tbsp (5 g) cayenne pepper

Preheat oven to 350°F (177°C).

Place all ingredients in a saucepan over high heat and bring to a boil. Cook until most of the liquid is gone, about 15 minutes. The mixture should be thick and syrupy. Be careful as the mixture will get extremely hot!

Remove from the heat and strain any liquid.

Put the pecans on a baking sheet lined with parchment paper, or a Silpat nonstick sheet, and bake for 15 to 20 minutes.

Allow the pecans to cool completely. They should have a hard candy crack to them. Break them up into pieces before using. You can store them in an airtight container at room temperature for up to 3 weeks.

Note

If you're not crazy about pecans, you can substitute walnuts in this recipe.

MEAD VINAIGRETTE

Salads may seem out of place during the colder months, but having a good dressing recipe in your repertoire will change everything. This dressing has a sweet-and-sour honey profile with a touch of herbaceous flavoring from the fresh chives and tanginess from the mustard, making it a great complement to many types of greens—especially the bitter ones. It may seem strange, but this vinaigrette is sweet enough to be drizzled over pound cakes or even ice cream.

YIELD: 8 TO 10 SERVINGS

MEAD REDUCTION

4 cups (946 ml) mead

½ cup (118 ml) honey

MEAD VINAIGRETTE

2 ounces (57 g) minced shallots

2 cups (473 ml) Mead Reduction

1 cup (237 ml) Champagne vinegar

2 cups (473 ml) canola oil

3 tbsp (47 g) Dijon mustard

1 tbsp (15 g) salt

1 tsp pepper

2 tbsp (6 g) chopped chives

Bring the mead and honey to a simmer in a saucepan over medium-high heat. Reduce by 75 percent, about 10 to 15 minutes. Cool completely before using.

To make the vinaigrette, add the shallots, Mead Reduction, vinegar, oil, mustard, salt and pepper to a blender and blend until completely emulsified. Whisk in the chopped chives. Store in an airtight container in the refrigerator until ready to use.

Note

Mead is a delicious honey wine that when reduced makes for a sweet, balanced vinaigrette. It can be substituted for any sweet dessert wine, such as *icewine*.

ROASTED MONKFISH WITH FARRO RISOTTO AND SAUTÉED BRUSSELS SPROUTS

New England is renowned for its seafood, and one of my favorite types is
the less commonly used monkfish. Monkfish is a dense, meaty and slightly sweet fish
with a taste that is similar to lobster tail. Adding the lemon juice to the cooked fillets brings
out a hint of acidity and the fresh flavor of the monkfish.

YIELD: 2 SERVINGS

2 (6 ounce [174 g]) monkfish fillets

1 tsp salt

½ tsp pepper

1 tsp lemon zest

3 tbsp (44 ml) canola oil

2 tbsp (30 ml) lemon juice

Farro Risotto (page 31)

Sautéed Brussels Sprouts (page 32)

Preheat oven to 400°F (204°C).

Season the monkfish fillets with salt, pepper and lemon zest.

Heat the canola oil in an oven-safe sauté pan over high heat until it begins to smoke. Add the monkfish fillets and sear until they are brown on both sides, about 8 to 10 minutes.

Finish cooking the fillets in the oven, uncovered, until they reach an internal temperature of 145°F (63°C), about 12 minutes. Allow the monkfish fillets to rest for 3 to 5 minutes and sprinkle with lemon juice before serving. Serve immediately with the risotto and Brussels sprouts.

Note

Ask your fishmonger if there are monkfish steaks with the bones left in—although they take a bit longer to cook, they yield more flavor. If fresh monkfish is not available, you can substitute swordfish or any other meaty fish.

FARRO RISOTTO

Farro is one of my favorite grains to eat during colder weather—it's especially substantial and it can accompany a variety of different proteins. I love this recipe in particular because it combines two of my favorite things: fat and hearty grains. The farro has an earthy, nutty flavor while the mascarpone adds a creamy richness—an unbeatable combo.

YIELD: 4 TO 6 SERVINGS

1 cup (237 ml) olive oil

2 large onions, diced

¼ cup (38 g) chopped garlic

3 cups (632 g) farro

1 cup (237 ml) white wine

4 cups (946 ml) Vegetable Stock (page 197)

2 bay leaves

½ bunch thyme sprigs

1 tbsp (15 g) salt

2 tsp (10 g) pepper

2 cups (483 g) mascarpone cheese

2 tbsp (5 g) chopped parsley

2 tbsp (6 g) chopped chives

Add the olive oil, onions and garlic to a saucepan over medium heat and sweat until tender, about 10 minutes. Add the uncooked farro to the pan and cook for 5 minutes to toast the grains. Add the white wine, stock, bay leaves, thyme, salt and pepper and cook until just tender, about 15 to 20 minutes.

Remove from heat and mix in the mascarpone cheese, parsley and chives. Serve immediately.

Note

This recipe works without the mascarpone, if you're looking for a dairy-free option.

SAUTÉED BRUSSELS SPROUTS

Fall is the best time to buy Brussels sprouts—it's when they're at the height of their season. I love Brussels sprouts and I especially love this recipe because it showcases a different way of preparing them. While the prep time is a little bit time consuming, the cooking time is incredibly fast so it all balances out. The spices and fat in this recipe help the Brussels sprouts truly shine— they're spicy, slightly bitter and tangy. Don't skip the lemon juice as it balances the spices and bitterness of the sprouts.

YIELD: 4 TO 6 SERVINGS

3 lbs (1.4 kg) Brussels sprouts

3 tbsp (44 ml) canola oil

1 tbsp (14 g) butter

¼ cup (60 g) sliced shallots

2 tsp (2 g) chili flakes

2 tsp (10 g) salt

1 tsp mustard seeds

2 tbsp (30 ml) freshly squeezed lemon juice

Prep the Brussels sprouts by cutting off the bottom a little at a time until you end up with loose leaves. Make your way all the down until only a small center is left. Set aside.

Heat a sauté pan over high heat and add the canola oil and butter. Add the shallots and cook for 1 minute. Add the Brussels sprout leaves, chili flakes, salt and mustard seeds. Cook for about 3 minutes, or until slightly tender. Add the lemon juice and serve immediately.

SEARED DUCK BREAST WITH PICKLED CRANBERRIES, CRANBERRY GASTRIQUE AND ROASTED CAULIFLOWER

Duck is one of those proteins that most people are intimidated to cook, but it's actually pretty painless to pull off. Duck meat is fatty and rich with a flavor that is similar to dark chicken meat. This rich, tart sauce packs an intense punch of cranberries—it's a perfect taste of fall in each bite! It's best to use it sparingly or serve it on the side so as not to overpower other flavors.

YIELD: 2 SERVINGS

2 (5–6 oz [145–174 g]) duck breasts

1 tsp salt

½ tsp pepper

CRANBERRY GASTRIQUE

6 cups (1.4 l) Chicken Stock (page 197)

4 cups (767 g) sugar

1 cup (237 ml) water

4 cups (946 ml) red wine vinegar

2 lbs (907 g) fresh cranberries

2 bay leaves

1 tbsp (15 g) salt

3 cups (710 ml) cranberry juice

Pickled Cranberries (page 36)
Roasted Cauliflower (page 39)

Make small score marks that look like Xs on the fatty side of the duck. Try to avoid cutting all the way down—past the fat—to the meat. Set aside.

Heat a sauté pan over high heat. Season the fatty side of the duck breasts with the salt and pepper and place in the pan, fat side down. Lower the heat to medium and allow the breasts to render out most of their fat, about 15 minutes. When the fat is mostly rendered, flip the duck breasts so that the meaty side is down, and cook for 2 more minutes. Remove from pan and allow to rest for 4 minutes before cutting into the breasts. Serve with Pickled Cranberries and Cranberry Gastrique.

CRANBERRY GASTRIQUE

In a large saucepan over medium-high heat, cook the chicken stock until it's reduced to 2 cups (473 ml), about 20 minutes. Set aside.

In a different saucepan, bring the sugar and water to a boil over high heat. Cook until the sugar begins to caramelize, about 10 to 15 minutes. Add the vinegar, cranberries, bay leaves, salt, cranberry juice and the reduced chicken stock. Cook until the mixture begins to thicken, about 10 minutes. Remove from heat.

Puree the mixture using a hand blender, or in batches if using a countertop blender. Add about ½ cup (118 ml) of water, as needed, to thin the mixture. Serve with pickled cranberries and cauliflower.

PICKLED CRANBERRIES

Growing up around cranberry bogs, I'm used to snacking on the tart and sour little berries. Pickling them, however, preserves the fruit and brings out its natural sweetness to balance out the tartness. Pickled Cranberries are such a staple in New England that they seem to be everywhere come fall. They're a great accompaniment for rich, fatty foods—think of all the holiday fare that's so perfectly balanced with a hint of cranberry sauce. They can also be a wonderful addition to salads.

YIELD: 4 CUPS (400 G)

1 cup (237 ml) red wine vinegar

1 ½ cups (302 g) brown sugar

¼ cup (60 g) salt

2 tbsp (17 g) black peppercorns

8 sprigs rosemary

1 tsp chili flakes

2 cups (473 ml) water

6 bay leaves

1 vanilla bean, split

2 lbs (907 g) fresh cranberries

Combine all ingredients, except the cranberries, into a saucepan and bring to a boil over high heat. Remove from the heat and allow to cool to room temperature.

Once cooled, pour the mixture over the cranberries. Cover tightly and let sit in the refrigerator for 1 to 2 days before using.

Pickled Cranberries will last for up to a month if stored in an airtight container in the refrigerator.

ROASTED CAULIFLOWER

Cauliflower is an underrated vegetable that gets a bad rap for being bland—so wrong! It's a universal vegetable that can go with just about anything, and is also great all on its own. When roasted until brown, the cauliflower develops an almost popcorn-like taste that's impossibly hard to resist.

YIELD: 8 SERVINGS

2 heads cauliflower

¼ cup (59 ml) canola oil

2 tsp (5 g) ground cumin

1 ½ tbsp (23 g) salt

½ tbsp (4 g) pepper

Preheat oven to 400°F (204°C).

Wash and cut off cauliflower florets from their stems. In a bowl, toss the cauliflower florets with canola oil, cumin, salt and pepper. Set aside.

Line a cookie sheet with foil and add the seasoned cauliflower in an even, single layer. Roast in the oven for 20 minutes. Serve immediately.

Note

Don't be afraid to use cauliflower of different colors if available; they all cook the same and the color contrast can actually enhance your meal. You also don't have to cut the florets off—you can quarter the cauliflower and roast the pieces by laying them on a sheet pan.

CIDER DOUGHNUTS WITH A CIDER GLAZE

Doughnuts are all about comfort. I think it's safe to say that we all keep a special place in our hearts for fried dough—with extra points if it's still warm and fresh out of the fryer. These cider doughnuts are extra comforting: they're rich, dense and spiced with cinnamon, nutmeg and ginger. They evoke brisk fall days and remind me of going to the local apple orchard to get cider doughnuts when I was a kid.

YIELD: 12 DOUGHNUTS

1 cup (190 g) granulated sugar

5 tbsp (75 g) unsalted butter, room temperature

2 eggs

3 ½ cups (350 g) all-purpose flour

1 ¼ tsp (8 g) salt

2 tsp (8 g) baking powder

1 tsp baking soda

1 ½ tsp (4 g) ground cinnamon

1 tsp ground ginger

½ tsp freshly grated nutmeg

½ cup (118 ml) buttermilk

⅓ cup (80 ml) apple cider

1 tbsp (15 ml) vanilla extract

CIDER GLAZE

4 cups (945 ml) apple cider

1 cup (237 ml) maple syrup

1 cup (130 g) powdered sugar

2 tsp (10 g) salt

Confectioner's sugar and/or cinnamon-sugar to coat doughnuts, optional

Using the paddle attachment for your stand mixer, beat the sugar and butter until pale and fluffy, about 4 to 6 minutes. Add the eggs, one at a time, beating a minute after each addition.

In a medium-size bowl, whisk together the flour, salt, baking powder, baking soda, cinnamon, ginger and nutmeg. Set aside.

Pour the buttermilk, cider and vanilla extract into the sugar/butter/egg mixture in the mixer. Thoroughly mix and then add the flour mixture. Combine gently until fully moistened.

Line two baking sheets with parchment paper and dust generously with flour. Turn the dough out onto one baking sheet and pat gently into ¾ inch (2 cm) thickness. Sprinkle the dough with additional flour, cover with plastic wrap and place in the refrigerator for 1 hour to firm up.

To make the glaze, reduce the apple cider and maple syrup in a saucepan over medium heat until it's thick and can coat the back of a spoon, about 10 minutes. Remove from heat and whisk in the powdered sugar and salt until fully incorporated. Set aside until ready to use.

Remove the dough from the refrigerator. Pick out two ring molds, and use them to cut the dough into desired sizes. Place the cut doughnuts on your second baking sheet as you go, then transfer to the refrigerator for 30 minutes to firm up again.

Line a plate with a few layers of paper towels and set it nearby. In a large pot, heat 3 inches (8 cm) of oil to 370°F (188°C). Drop 3 or 4 doughnuts into the oil, being careful not to crowd the pan. Cook until browned on one side, about 1 minute; then flip and cook until browned on the other side, about 1 minute longer. Repeat with the remaining dough—if you find that it's getting too soft as you work your way through the batches, cool the dough in the refrigerator. When the doughnuts are cool enough to handle but still warm, sprinkle all over with cinnamon sugar or confectioners' sugar. Serve immediately with Cider Glaze.

WALNUT BROWN BUTTER CAKE WITH ROASTED APPLES AND SALTED CARAMEL

This cake is reminiscent of an angel food cake because it's so irresistibly light and fluffy. The brown butter makes it extra rich and adds a deep nuttiness that complements the toasted walnuts perfectly. I love to make this recipe in the fall because it pairs so well with fall fruits. While this recipe is served with Roasted Apples (page 44), pears, plums and even late summer berries are also delicious with it.

YIELD: 8 TO 10 SERVINGS

1 ¼ cups (145 g) chopped walnuts

1 lb (454 g) butter, plus some more melted butter for coating the cake pan

1 vanilla bean

1 ⅓ cups (174 g) powdered sugar

⅓ cup (30 g) cake flour

2 tsp (10 g) salt

6 egg whites

3 tbsp (36 g) granulated sugar

Roasted Apples (page 44)

Salted Caramel (page 44)

Preheat the oven to 350°F (177°C).

Spread the walnuts on a baking sheet and toast for 12 to 15 minutes, until they're golden brown and smell nutty. Set aside to cool.

Cut out a circle of parchment paper to fit the bottom of a 10 inch (25 cm) round cake pan. Brush the pan with enough melted butter to coat the bottom and then line it with the cut-out parchment paper.

Place a pound (454 g) of butter in a medium saucepan. Split the vanilla bean lengthwise down the center and add it to the saucepan with the butter. Cook over medium heat until the butter browns, about 6 to 8 minutes. Remove from heat and allow to cool. Once cooled remove the vanilla bean and discard.

Pulse the walnuts and powdered sugar in a food processor until finely ground. Add the flour and salt and pulse to combine. Transfer to a large bowl.

Place the egg whites in the bowl of a KitchenAid® stand mixer, fitted with the whisk attachment. Add the granulated sugar and mix on high for 4 to 5 minutes, or until the mixture forms very stiff peaks. When you turn the whisk upside down, the peaks should hold.

Alternate between folding the egg whites and the brown butter into the dry ingredients, about a third of each at a time.

Once combined, add the batter into the prepared cake pan and bake for 50 minutes to 1 hour. Remove from the oven and cool on a rack for 30 minutes. Run a knife around the edge of the pan and invert the cake onto a plate. Peel off the parchment and turn the cake back onto a serving platter. Top with Roasted Apples and the caramel.

SALTED CARAMEL

Ah, Salted Caramel! Who doesn't love you? You're everything I love about traditional, sweet caramel but with a touch of salt that balances out the sweetness. I definitely prefer Salted Caramel to the nonsalted kind, but you can happily omit the salt for the traditional sauce.

YIELD: 6 TO 8 SERVINGS

2 cups (383 g) granulated sugar

1 cup (237 ml) water

12 tbsp (172 g) unsalted butter, cubed and at room temperature

1 cup (237 ml) heavy cream, at room temperature

1 tbsp (10 g) fleur de sel, or any other kind of flaky sea salt

Add the sugar and water to a medium heavy-bottomed saucepan. Heat over medium-high heat for about 8 to 10 minutes, or until the sugar reaches a deep amber color. It should look almost reddish-brown. This is the point where the caramel can go from perfect to burnt in a matter of seconds, so keep a close eye on it! If you're using an instant-read thermometer, cook the sugar until it reaches 350°F (177°C).

As soon as the caramel reaches 350°F (177°C), add the butter all at once. Be careful, as the mixture will bubble up when the butter is added. Whisk the butter into the caramel until it's completely melted.

Remove from heat and slowly pour the cream into the caramel. Again, be careful because it will bubble up. Whisk until all of the cream has been incorporated and the sauce is smooth. Add the fleur de sel and whisk to combine.

Use right away or allow the sauce to cool prior to storing in an airtight container. Sauce will last for up to 2 weeks in the refrigerator.

ROASTED APPLES

This simple recipe embodies all the cozy warmth of fall. It's like apple pie, minus the tricky pie dough part.

YIELD: 4 SERVINGS

¼ cup (50 g) brown sugar

½ tsp ground cinnamon

½ tsp ground allspice

1 tsp salt

4 Honeycrisp apples

2 tbsp (30 ml) olive oil

Preheat the oven to 400°F (205°C).

Mix the brown sugar, cinnamon, allspice and salt together. Set aside.

Cut the apples in half and remove the core. Cut in half again. Place the apples on a foil-lined cookie sheet and drizzle the olive oil over them. Sprinkle the sugar mixture over the apples. Roast in the preheated oven until tender and slightly caramelized, about 30 minutes.

MUSHROOM RISOTTO WITH CABERNET VINEGAR REDUCTION

This rich dish highlights the delicious earthiness of mushrooms. It's perfectly good by itself or a great complement to chicken, pork or beef. The reduction's the perfect combination of sweet and sour, and it definitely doesn't take much to pack a punch. Be careful not to use too much, since its acidity can overpower other flavors.

YIELD: 8 TO 10 SERVINGS

½ cup (76 g) chopped garlic

2 cups (303 g) diced onions

¼ cup (59 ml) canola oil

½ lb (227 g) shiitake mushrooms, with the stems removed

¼ lb (113 g) button mushrooms, with the stems removed and sliced

¼ lb (113 g) oyster mushrooms, with the stems removed

1 cup (237 ml) white wine

3 cups (632 g) arborio rice

5 cups (1 l) Mushroom Stock (page 198), simmering hot

10 tbsp (143 g) cold butter, cubed

1 ½ cups (270 g) grated Pecorino cheese

1 tbsp (3 g) thyme leaves

2 tbps (30 g) salt

2 tsp (10 g) pepper

CABERNET VINEGAR REDUCTION

16 oz (454 ml) Cabernet vinegar

¼ cup (48 g) sugar

1 tbsp (8 g) black peppercorns

2 sprigs fresh rosemary

Heat a rondeau pan, or any other wide and shallow pot, over high heat. Add the canola oil, garlic, onions and mushrooms. Cook over high heat until the garlic and onions soften and the mushrooms begin to caramelize, about 12 minutes.

Add the arborio rice to the pan and toast for 3 minutes. Add the white wine and stir the rice continuously. You don't want to walk away from the rice at this point! It needs to be constantly stirred or your finished dish will be lumpy and unevenly cooked.

Once the rice has absorbed all of the wine, about 4 to 5 minutes, begin adding the stock, 1 cup (240 ml) at a time. Continue stirring. Once the rice absorbs the stock and starts to look dry, add another cup of stock until you finish the stock. The rice should double in size. Taste the rice to make sure it's done. It should be al dente.

Remove from the heat and add the cold butter, Pecorino cheese, thyme, salt and pepper. Finish the risotto by drizzling some Cabernet Vinegar Reduction over the top.

To make the reduction, add all of the ingredients to a saucepan and bring to a simmer over medium heat until the liquid is reduced by half and begins to get syrupy, about 15 to 20 minutes. Remove from the heat and strain out the peppercorns and rosemary. Cool completely before using.

Reduction will last for a month at room temperature, as long as it's covered.

SPICY CHORIZO AND CLAM CHOWDER

This wouldn't be a New England cookbook without a recipe for clam chowder! But this isn't your grandma's chowder; it's a subtle spin on the classic. It beautifully celebrates the flavors from the land and sea in a rich, creamy and spicy chowder that's ideal on a cold day. The spiciness of the chorizo and Tabasco® bring out the clam flavor quite well.

YIELD: 4 TO 6 SERVINGS

1 lb (500 g) chorizo, diced

2 cups (303 g) diced onions

¼ cup (38 g) chopped garlic

1 cup (151 g) diced celery

1 cup (151 g) diced carrots

1 cup (230 g) butter

1 cup (125 g) flour

4 cups (946 ml) cream

2 cups (473 ml) clam juice

2 tbsp (30 ml) Tabasco® sauce

2 cups (360 g) diced Idaho potatoes

3 cups (724 g) clams, shucked and chopped

1 lemon, juiced and zested

1 ½ tbsp (5 g) fresh thyme leaves

1 ½ tbsp (23 g) salt

2 tsp (10 g) pepper

3 tbsp (8 g) fresh parsley leaves, chopped

Heat a stockpot over medium heat and add the chorizo, onions and garlic. Cook until the chorizo starts to render out some of its fat and the onions become translucent, about 10 minutes. Add the celery and carrots and cook for 5 minutes. Next, add the butter and flour and cook for 5 more minutes.

Add the cream, clam juice, Tabasco® and potatoes. Cook over medium heat until the potatoes are tender, about 10 to 12 minutes. Add the clams, lemon juice, lemon zest, thyme, salt and pepper. Cook for 7 minutes.

Garnish each serving with chopped parsley.

Note

Traditional clam chowder is made with fatback or bacon, and either can be substituted for the chorizo in this recipe. You can make this chowder gluten-free by simply omitting the flour. While it won't be as thick, it'll still be delicious.

BIBB LETTUCE WITH FRESH APPLES, BANYULS BROWN BUTTER VINAIGRETTE AND FRIED SUNCHOKE CHIPS

This salad is an all-around winner. It's sweet and sour combined with a rounded-out butteriness and nuttiness, thanks to our good friend brown butter. The apples give it a fresh crunch and sourness that pairs so well with the fatty vinaigrette. I really love this dish because it happens to be refreshing and rich all at once, and very satisfying.

YIELD: 4 SERVINGS

1 head Bibb lettuce

1 Granny Smith apple, julienned

¼ of a red onion, julienned

½ cup (56 g) Fried Sunchoke Chips (page 53)

¼ cup (59 ml) Banyuls Brown Butter Vinaigrette (page 52)

Pick apart the leaves from the head of the Bibb lettuce and gently rinse under cold water. Pat dry or use a salad spinner.

In a large bowl, gently mix the lettuce, apples, onions and the vinaigrette. Top with the Fried Sunchoke Chips prior to serving.

BANYULS BROWN BUTTER VINAIGRETTE

Banyuls is a sweet wine from a region of France that borders Spain. It has a slightly sweet and nutty flavor that, when combined with brown butter, makes a rich and savory dressing that's great for a chilly day salad. It has the perfect balance of acidity from the vinegar and toasted nuttiness from the brown butter.

YIELD: 10 TO 12 SERVINGS

½ lb (227 g) butter

¼ cup (50 g) minced shallots

¾ cup (177 ml) Banyuls vinegar

¾ cup (177 ml) canola oil

½ cup (118 ml) olive oil

3 tbsp (45 ml) honey

3 tbsp (47 ml) whole grain mustard

½ tbsp (2 g) fresh thyme leaves

2 tsp (10 g) salt

½ tsp pepper

In a medium saucepan, bring the butter and shallots to a simmer over medium-high heat. Once the butter turns light brown and begins to get foamy, about 10 minutes, remove from the heat and set aside to cool to room temperature.

Combine the Banyuls vinegar, canola and olive oils. Set aside.

Add the butter and shallot mixture to a blender along with the honey, mustard, thyme, salt and pepper and blend for 3 minutes, until fully combined. Slowly drizzle in the oil mixture until the vinaigrette is completely emulsified.

Vinaigrette will last up to a week if refrigerated in an airtight container. When using it after being refrigerated, let sit for an hour to bring to room temperature, or microwave in 30-second increments until the butter is fully melted and blend to re-emulsify.

Note

If you can't find Banyuls, sherry vinegar is a good substitute.

FRIED SUNCHOKE CHIPS

Sunchokes, also known as Jerusalem artichokes, are a root vegetable that resembles the potato. Once fried, they're somewhat sweet, earthy and crunchy. I like them as a hearty addition to most salads, but they're great on their own, too.

YIELD: 4 SERVINGS

¼ lb (113 g) sunchokes

4 cups (946 ml) canola oil

Salt, as needed

Thinly slice the sunchokes and keep submerged in cold water.

Heat the canola oil in a large pot over medium heat until it reaches 325°F (163°C).

When the oil is ready, dry the sliced sunchokes on paper towels. This step is very important! Too much water introduced to hot oil can be dangerous.

Fry the sunchokes, 12 to 15 at a time, in the oil until golden brown. Once fried, place them on paper towels to remove the excess oil.

Season to taste with salt.

BRAISED VEAL OSSO BUCO WITH CREAMY POLENTA AND CARAMELIZED OYSTER MUSHROOMS

Whenever the weather starts to get chilly, I immediately begin to crave braised meats. This menu is comfort food at its finest, and it's the perfect meal to warm you up. The combined warmth of the star anise and richness of the veal make for a decadent fall meal.

YIELD: 6 SERVINGS

6 (1 lb [454 g]) veal osso buco

3 tbsp (45 g) salt

1 tbsp (15 g) pepper

¼ cup (59 ml) canola oil

3 lbs (1.4 kg) chopped carrots

5 onions, sliced

3 cups (454 g) chopped celery

1 cup (161 g) garlic, whole

1 oz (28 g) rosemary sprigs

1 oz (28 g) thyme sprigs

6 bay leaves

2 star anise

2 tbsp (17 g) black peppercorns

2 ½ cups (592 ml) white wine

4 quarts (3.8 l) Chicken Stock (page 197)

Creamy Polenta (page 57)

Caramelized Oyster Mushrooms (page 57)

Season the osso buco with salt and pepper. In a rondeau, or a wide and shallow pan, sear the osso buco in canola oil until dark brown, 12–15 minutes. Rest osso buco on a baking sheet and set aside.

In the same rondeau you used to sear the osso buco, sweat the carrots, onions and celery for 8 to 10 minutes over medium-high heat. Add the garlic, rosemary, thyme, bay leaves, anise, black peppercorns and white wine. Cook until the wine is reduced by half, about 12 minutes.

Add the stock and bring to a boil. Turn the heat to medium-low and return the osso buco back into the pot. Cook, covered, until the osso buco is fork-tender, about 6 hours. When the osso buco is tender, remove it from the pot and allow it to rest for 15 minutes.

Strain the braising liquid and discard any solids. Bring it back to a boil and reduce it by half, until it starts to get thick, 15 to 20 minutes. Add the osso buco back into the reduced braising liquid and serve with the polenta and the mushrooms.

CREAMY POLENTA

Polenta is the perfect vehicle for any saucy dish. It happily soaks up any sauces or juices and immediately enhances the taste. It has the subtle sweetness of corn, but it's still savory and rich. The fontina cheese makes the polenta even more rich and gooey, so don't skimp on it!

YIELD: 4 TO 6 SERVINGS

¼ cup (50 g) minced shallots

2 tbsp (19 g) minced garlic

6 tbsp (86 g) butter

2 cups (473 ml) milk

2 cups (473 ml) water

1 cup (170 g) polenta or coarse cornmeal

1 cup (180 g) grated fontina cheese

2 tsp (10 g) salt

½ tsp pepper

In a saucepan over medium heat, sweat the shallots and garlic in 2 tablespoons (29 g) of butter until tender, about 5 minutes. Add the milk and cook on medium heat.

In a separate bowl, whisk the water and polenta together. Add it to the saucepan and stir constantly, while still cooking on medium heat. The polenta should start to thicken as it cooks. Once the polenta is thick enough to coat your spoon, about 15 minutes, remove it from the heat and stir in the remaining butter along with the cheese, salt and pepper.

CARAMELIZED OYSTER MUSHROOMS

Oyster mushrooms are thin and delicately flavored. They're earthy and have an almost caramel flavor when cooked until they're slightly crispy, as they are in this recipe. They won't overpower a dish, but instead add another layer of flavor that is addictive. Because they are so delicate, they don't need to be cooked for long and are perfect for any quick sauté or stir-fry meal.

YIELD: 4 TO 6 SERVINGS

1 lb (454 g) oyster mushrooms

2 tbsp (30 ml) canola oil

¼ cup (50 g) minced shallots

2 tbsp (29 g) butter

1 ½ tsp (8 g) salt

¼ tsp pepper

3 tbsp (9 g) minced chives

Clean all oyster mushrooms by removing their stems and ripping them in half if they're large.

Heat a large sauté pan over high heat and add the canola oil and cleaned mushrooms. Cook on high until the mushrooms begin to caramelize and get crispy, about 5 to 8 minutes. Lower the heat to medium and add the shallots, butter, salt and pepper. Cook for 5 minutes. Remove from the heat and toss in the fresh chives. Serve immediately.

ROASTED COD WITH CREAMY SUCCOTASH

I like the delicate flavor of cod and haddock, as long as they're fresh. Make sure to visit your local fish market for the freshest option, rather than buying it in bulk. The succotash also makes this dish very fall-appropriate and is a nice contrast to the sweet corn and slightly acidic cherry tomatoes.

YIELD: 4 SERVINGS

2 tbsp (30 ml) canola oil

1 ½ lbs (680 g) cod or haddock fillets, cut into 6-oz (170-g) pieces

Salt as needed

Pepper as needed

2 tbsp (30 ml) fresh lemon juice

CREAMY SUCCOTASH

4 cups (946 ml) water

1 cup (151 g) lima beans

1 cup (201 g) small-dice potatoes

2 tbsp (30 ml) canola oil

1 cup (151 g) diced Spanish onions

2 tbsp (19 g) chopped garlic

1 ½ tbsp (14 g) minced jalapeños

1 cup (151 g) diced red bell peppers

1 cup (151 g) shucked corn

1 cup (161 g) cherry tomatoes, cut in half

½ cup (118 ml) heavy cream

1 tsp salt

¼ tsp pepper

2 tbsp (5 g) chopped parsley

2 tsp (6 g) lemon zest

Preheat oven to 400°F (205°C).

Heat a sauté or cast iron pan over high heat and add the canola oil. Pat the fish fillets dry with a paper towel and season with salt and pepper. Immediately after seasoning, sear the fillets in the hot pan. If you season the fillets too early, the salt will pull moisture out of the fish and there'll be a greater chance of the fillets sticking to the pan and of not getting a nice, brown sear.

Sear the fillet on one side until brown, about 2 to 3 minutes per side, then flip and repeat. Sprinkle lemon juice over the fillets and finish in the preheated oven. Bake for 10 to 12 minutes. Allow the fillets to rest for 3 minutes before serving with the succotash.

To make the succotash, bring 4 cups (946 ml) of water to a boil. Blanch the lima beans until tender, 3 minutes. Remove from the water and set aside. Blanch the potatoes in the same boiling water until tender, 4–5 minutes. Remove from the water and set aside.

Heat a large sauté pan over high heat. Add the canola oil, onions, garlic, jalapeño and bell peppers and cook until tender, about 4 to 5 minutes. Add the corn and blanched potatoes and cook for 3 minutes. Add the cherry tomatoes, blanched lima beans, heavy cream, salt and pepper and cook until the heavy cream has reduced to the point of just glazing the vegetables. Remove from heat. Toss in the parsley and lemon zest. Serve while hot.

PUMPKIN PANNA COTTA WITH CINNAMON WHIPPED CREAM AND HONEYCOMB CANDY

Chinese five-spice powder is composed of star anise, cloves, cinnamon,
Sichuan peppercorns and fennel. Such a wild spice combination may seem odd for a dessert recipe,
but it actually makes this panna cotta stand out from the traditional sweet fare. The spices bring out
the warm pumpkin flavor that goes so well with cozy fall days.

YIELD: 10 SERVINGS

1 ¼ cups (275 g) pumpkin puree

½ cup (101 g) brown sugar

½ tsp salt

1 tsp Chinese five-spice powder

2 ½ cups (592 ml) milk

4 tsp (18 g) gelatin

Cinnamon Whipped Cream
(page 62)

Honeycomb Candy (page 62)

In a blender, add the pumpkin puree, brown sugar, salt, Chinese five-spice powder and 1 ½ cups (355 g) of the milk. Blend until smooth.

In a saucepan, heat the remaining milk and gelatin until the gelatin is completely dissolved.

Add the blended pumpkin mixture to the saucepan with the gelatin and gently cook on medium heat until it reaches 180°F (82°C), or it just begins to lightly simmer.

Remove from heat and pour into 6-ounce (170-g) ramekins. Allow to chill in the refrigerator for about 5 hours before serving. Serve with a dollop of Cinnamon Whipped Cream and chunks of Honeycomb Candy.

Note

Using canned pumpkin puree for this recipe is perfectly fine. I would actually not recommend roasting a whole pumpkin for the small amount of puree that's needed, but if you do, the leftover puree can be stored in the refrigerator and used for anything your heart desires.

HONEYCOMB CANDY

Honeycomb candy is so much fun to make and it's actually way easier than most people think.
The end result is a sweet, fluffy and crunchy candy that's addictive.

YIELD: 10 TO 12 SERVINGS

1 ½ cups (288 g) sugar

½ cup (118 ml) water

3 tbsp (45 ml) honey

⅓ cup (79 ml) corn syrup

4 tsp (17 g) baking soda, sifted

In a large saucepan over medium heat, whisk together the sugar, water, honey and corn syrup. Boil until the mixture is amber-colored and the sugar begins to look like caramel, about 10 minutes. Add the baking soda and, with a wooden spoon, stir gently. It will foam up a lot; don't worry!

Pour the mixture onto a sheet pan covered with Silpat® or parchment paper. Allow to cool for 20 minutes. Once cooled, break into chunks. Candy can be stored in an airtight jar at room temperature for up to a month.

CINNAMON WHIPPED CREAM

This recipe is for your classic, go-to whipped cream with a lovely twist: cinnamon.
The warmth of cinnamon turns the whipped cream into a perfect topping for fall desserts.

YIELD: 8 SERVINGS

1 cup (237 ml) cold heavy whipping cream

1 tsp vanilla extract

2 ½ tbsp (20 g) powdered sugar

1 ½ tsp (4 g) ground cinnamon

Add all of the ingredients to the bowl of a KitchenAid® stand mixer with the whisk attachment. Whisk on medium speed until peaks form, about 5 to 7 minutes.

Whipped cream is best served on the day it's made, but it can be stored in the refrigerator for a day.

Note

To yield fluffy whipped cream, it's important to make sure the cream is very cold when you whip it. It helps to move quickly when making this recipe. Be careful not to overwhip the cream, as it will separate and turn somewhat greasy.

Winter

When the colder weather arrives, cravings for hearty, rich and decadent meals arise—meals that warm you right up and ease the pain of the cold. This chapter is filled with slow-cooked, fatty and generous recipes to comfort you throughout the frigid days. Winter is indeed a delicious time!

The lower the temperature dips, the longer your oven and stovetop should stay on. Recipes with lengthy cooking times are never more welcome than in the wintertime. 'Tis the season for braises, stews and soups. There's nothing better than staying in your warm house during a snow day, watching the snow fall while drinking hot cocoa and cooking up a storm. These recipes are meant for those cozy days. They embrace the bounty of the season, making the most of root vegetables that are naturally hearty. They celebrate beautiful cuts of meat with dishes that are sure to satisfy your most carnivorous cravings. They'll keep you warm all season and, when you just can't stand the cold anymore, you'll have citrus to hold you over until spring. Winter is the time for citrus harvests and this chapter is sprinkled with citrus-centric recipes that'll give you hope for warmer days.

These menus are also great for entertaining. With lots of holiday gatherings during this time, these recipes are ideal for impressing house guests. From elaborate meals to simpler dishes, this chapter has it all to keep you cooking until spring.

PORK BELLY WITH BRAISED PINE NUTS AND ROASTED QUINCE

I love this recipe because I love roasted pork belly; it's as simple as that. Most people shy away from its jiggly fat, but I think it's the tastiest part of the cut. The fat also helps the meat become tender and soft when cooked. Pork belly is rich, with a somewhat intensified pork flavor because of its high fat content.

YIELD: 12 SERVINGS

¼ cup (50 g) brown sugar

3 tbsp (45 g) salt

½ tsp pepper

1 tsp ground fennel

1 tsp ground cumin

2 tsp (5 g) ground ginger

2 lbs (907 g) pork belly

Braised Pine Nuts (page 68)
Roasted Quince (page 68)

Mix the brown sugar, salt, pepper, fennel, cumin and ginger and rub on top of the pork belly. Allow to cure, uncovered, in the refrigerator for 24 to 48 hours.

After curing the pork belly, rinse off the spices and pat dry with paper towels.

Preheat the oven to 450°F (232°C).

Place the pork belly in a roasting pan and roast for 20 minutes, then without removing the pan from the oven, turn the temperature down to 300°F (149°C) and continue cooking for another 2 hours.

The pork belly should be tender and its fat gelatinous when done. Aim for an internal temperature of 165°F (74°C). Serve topped with the pine nuts and Roasted Quince.

Note

I recommend getting a pork belly without the skin. I personally prefer to use one with skin, but the skin needs to be scored with a knife in a very detailed way otherwise it becomes too crunchy and hard to eat. Do not trim any of the fat off the pork belly before cooking. Remember, fat is flavor!

BRAISED PINE NUTS

This recipe offers some complex flavors with the savoriness of the nuts
and the slight sweetness from the sherry wine—it's delicious.

YIELD: 6 TO 8 SERVINGS

½ lb (227 g) butter

2 cups (251 g) pine nuts

¼ cup (38 g) chopped garlic

2 tbsp (29 g) diced ginger

2 tbsp (19 g) diced jalapeños

1 cup (151 g) diced onions

1 cup (151 g) diced carrots

1 ½ cups (255 ml) sherry wine

4 cups (946 ml) Chicken Stock
(page 197)

2 tsp (2 g) chopped rosemary

1 tbsp (15 g) salt

2 tsp (10 g) pepper

Heat a large saucepan over medium heat. Add the butter and pine nuts and
toast until golden brown, 4 to 5 minutes. Add the garlic, ginger and jalapeños
and cook for 5 minutes. Add the onions, carrots and sherry wine and cook
for 10 minutes, or until the wine is reduced to about ½ cup (118 ml). Add
the chicken stock, rosemary, salt and pepper and cook for 15 to 20 minutes.
When done, the pine nuts should be thick and saucy, almost like baked beans.

ROASTED QUINCE

Quince is typically found in New England from the beginning of fall to right around the New Year.
The honey offers an earthy sweetness that's absolutely delicious.

YIELD: 8 SERVINGS

4 cups (946 ml) water

½ cup (118 ml) lemon juice

4 quince

2 ½ cups (592 ml) Riesling wine

½ cup (118 ml) Champagne vinegar

2 tsp (10 g) salt

½ tsp chili flakes

4 tbsp (60 ml) honey

8 thyme sprigs

Preheat the oven to 375°F (191°C).

Mix the water and lemon juice in a large bowl. Cut the quince into quarters,
remove its core and peel the skin off. Immediately drop into the bowl with
lemon water.

Once cleaned, put the quince into a glass baking dish. Discard lemon water.
Pour the wine, vinegar, salt and chili flakes over it. Drizzle the honey over the
quince and add the thyme. Bake, uncovered, for 30 minutes in the preheated
oven. Flip the quince so that the once-exposed side gets to cook in the wine
and bake for another 30 minutes.

FRESH PASTA WITH BOLOGNESE SAUCE

When I was growing up, my mom often made spaghetti and meatballs, so I have a soft spot for fresh pasta dinners. It might seem intimidating to make your own pasta, but it's incredibly easy and once you learn you'll have a hard time going back to the dry, boxed stuff. Bolognese sauce is traditionally made with ground beef and pork, but I like swapping the pork for lamb because it adds a more interesting flavor.

YIELD: 12 TO 20 SERVINGS

4 cups (700 g) semolina flour, plus some extra to prevent pasta from sticking

4 eggs

2 egg yolks

¼ cup (59 ml) olive oil

¼ cup (59 ml) water

2 tsp (10 g) salt

1 tsp pepper

½ cup (63 g) flour, plus more for dusting your rolling surface

BOLOGNESE SAUCE

Canola oil

2 lbs (907 g) ground beef

2 lbs (907 g) ground lamb

1 ½ tbsp (2 g) dry oregano

2 tsp (1 g) chili flakes

1 ½ tbsp (23 g) salt

¼ cup (38 g) chopped garlic

2 cups (303 g) finely diced onions

1 cup (151 g) finely diced carrots

3 cups (710 ml) red wine

2 cups (473 ml) Chicken Stock (page 197)

4 cups (990 g) canned tomatoes

2 sprigs rosemary

½ cup (25 g) basil

2 tbsp (5 g) thyme

1 bay leaf

Using a KitchenAid® stand mixer with the dough-hook attachment, mix all ingredients, except the sauce, on low speed until they begin to form a ball, about 12 to 14 minutes. Remove dough and flatten it as much as possible with your hands, so it looks like a disk. Wrap the dough in plastic wrap and allow to rest for 30 minutes at room temperature.

Cut the dough into six pieces. On a lightly floured surface, roll out the dough to ⅟₁₆ of an inch (1.6 mm). You can do this by hand but I recommend using KitchenAid® pasta attachments for the stand mixer. Cut the pasta into desired shapes, such as long strips for pappardelle or tagliatelle. To make bow ties, cut the pasta into small squares and pinch the middle. Use extra semolina flour to keep the pasta from sticking and store in the refrigerator until the sauce is ready. To cook the pasta, boil water and cook the pasta until it floats and is al dente. Cooking time varies by shape, so keep an eye on it.

To make the sauce, heat a large saucepan over high heat. Add enough canola oil to just cover the bottom of the pan. Add the beef, lamb, oregano, chili flakes and salt. Cook until the fat begins to render, about 12 to 15 minutes. Add the garlic, onions and carrots. Cook for 5 minutes. Add the red wine and chicken stock, and simmer for 15 minutes. Add the tomatoes and herbs. You can extract the bay leaf, but I find that as the sauce sits it extracts more flavor. Simmer for 4 hours over low heat. Remove from heat and serve immediately with the pasta.

LOBSTER AND CELERY ROOT BISQUE

This is the ultimate luxurious lobster bisque: It's silky and packed with tons of lobster flavor. The addition of celery root, a fantastic winter root vegetable, adds an earthy sweetness. I also like this recipe because it celebrates fresh New England lobster and uses every bit of lobster meat. Fresh live lobster is what makes this bisque so flavorful. Don't buy already shucked lobster meat—it simply won't compare.

YIELD: 6 SERVINGS

4 (1 ¼ lb [567 g]) lobsters

2 tbsp (30 ml) canola oil

2 onions, roughly chopped

5 garlic cloves

3 tbsp (23 g) tomato paste

½ head fennel, sliced

2 tbsp (17 g) peppercorns

2 cups (473 ml) sherry wine

1 orange peel

3 bay leaves

3 quarts (2.8 l) heavy cream

2 quarts (1.8 l) half-and-half

2 lbs (907 g) celery root, peeled and diced

1 tbsp + 1 tsp (20 g) salt

8 tbsp (115 g) butter

Bring a pot of water to a boil.

Insert a knife into the head of each lobster and split it. Remove the heads and set them aside for the broth. Place the tails in a large bowl and the claws in a different large bowl.

Pour enough of the boiling water to cover the lobster tails and let sit for 6 minutes. Do the same to the claws and let sit for 8 minutes. After their allotted time, remove the tails and claws from the water and crack their shells to release the meat. It takes plenty of practice to remove the meat in one piece, so don't worry if it's not the prettiest-looking meat.

Cut the tail meat in half and then again into cubes. The claws can also be cut, but I usually leave those whole for garnish. Allow the meat to chill in the refrigerator.

Heat a large stockpot over high heat. Add the canola oil and lobster heads. Roast the heads in the pot until they start to brown, 5 to 8 minutes. Add the onion, garlic, tomato paste, fennel and peppercorns and cook for 10 minutes. Add the sherry, orange peel and bay leaves and cook for 8 to 10 minutes, or until most of the wine is gone. Add the heavy cream and half-and-half. Bring to a boil, then turn it down to a simmer.

Simmer for 40 minutes, then strain the vegetables and lobster heads. Return the lobster cream to the pot and add the diced celery root and salt. Cook until the celery root is tender. Once tender, add the cream and celery root to a blender in batches. Blend until smooth.

Melt the butter in a small saucepan. Add the chilled lobster meat and gently warm it up over low heat.

To serve, ladle the soup into bowls and garnish with the buttered lobster meat.

ARUGULA SALAD WITH ALMONDS, GREEN OLIVES AND BLOOD ORANGE

This salad is a refreshing break from all the hearty winter fare; better yet, it's the perfect accompaniment to rich and heavy foods. It's fresh and light but still manages to celebrate the season with blood oranges, which are only ripe during the wintertime. This beautiful variety of orange has just the right amount of acidity so that it replaces the need for a classic salad dressing. The peppery arugula is mellowed out by the blood orange and the briny olives, with a nice crunch added by the buttery almonds. Not only delicious, this impressive salad is also extremely easy to put together.

YIELD: 4 SERVINGS

½ cup (80 g) sliced almonds

3 cups (145 g) arugula, washed and dried

¾ cup (135 g) Cerignola or Picholine green olives, pits removed and sliced

1 blood orange, segmented (you'll need only 4 segments)

4 tbsp (59 ml) olive oil

1 tbsp (15 g) sea salt

Preheat the oven to 350°F (177°C).

Toast the almonds on a cookie sheet for 5 to 7 minutes, or until golden brown. Allow to cool.

Cut any unwanted stems from the arugula and discard.

Toss all ingredients together and serve.

BRAISED PORK SHANKS WITH SPINACH DUMPLINGS AND GARLIC CHIPS

Pork shanks are an underrated cut of meat, but they have a fantastic porky flavor and they're actually pretty lean—the best of both worlds. After hours of braising, the pork is tender and warmly flavored by the apples, ginger, star anise and cinnamon. Their Flintstones-approved size makes them immediately impressive, so they're perfect for entertaining. If you happen to have any leftovers, just pick the pork off the bone and put it back into the glaze; you'll have a great sauce for pasta or polenta.

YIELD: 4 SERVINGS

4 (1 to 1 ½ lb [454 to 680 g]) pork shanks

2 tsp (5 g) ground cumin

1 ½ tbsp (23 g) salt

1 tsp pepper

¼ cup (59 ml) canola oil

4 onions, sliced

3 green apples, with their cores removed

12 garlic cloves, peeled

¼ lb (113 g) ginger, sliced

4 (16 oz [473 ml]) bottles of winter lager beer

10 cups (2.4 l) Chicken Stock (page 197)

4 star anise

1 cinnamon stick

Spinach Dumplings (page 79)

Garlic Chips (page 79)

Preheat the oven to 350°F (177°C).

Season each pork shank with cumin, salt and pepper.

Heat a rondeau, or a wide and shallow pot, on high heat. Add the canola oil and sear the pork shanks until brown on all sides, 8 minutes. Place in a braising pan and set aside.

In the same rondeau, sauté the onions, apples, garlic and ginger until they begin to caramelize, about 8 to 10 minutes. Deglaze the pan with the beer and cook until it's almost reduced completely, 10 to 12 minutes.

Add the chicken stock, star anise and cinnamon stick and bring to a boil. Cook for 15 minutes. Remove from the heat and carefully pour the liquid over the pork shanks in the braising pan. Cover and cook in the preheated oven for 3 hours.

After 3 hours, check the shanks to make sure they're tender. If they aren't tender enough, cook for another 45 minutes. Their internal temperature should be 165°F (74°C) when done. Take the braising pan out of the oven and carefully remove the shanks. Set aside and allow them to rest, 15 to 20 minutes.

Strain the braising liquid to remove any solids. In a stockpot, bring the liquid to a boil and cook for 20 to 25 minutes until it's reduced to a glaze. Add the shanks to the stockpot to warm them up. Serve immediately with the dumplings and garlic chips.

SPINACH DUMPLINGS

These dumplings are light pillows of pure goodness! The delicate spinach flavor pairs very well with the salty parmesan cheese, and they can be served with whatever sauce your heart desires.

YIELD: 8 TO 10 SERVINGS

1 lb (454 g) fresh ricotta

1 lb (454 g) spinach

½ cup (90 g) grated Parmesan cheese

4 egg yolks

1 egg

1 tbsp (15 g) salt

½ tsp pepper

½ tsp grated nutmeg

½ cup (63 g) flour

Strain the ricotta overnight in the refrigerator to get as much moisture out of it as possible. Bring a pot of water to a boil. Fill a large bowl with water and ice, and set aside. Remove the stems from the spinach and discard. Blanch the spinach leaves in the boiling water for 2 minutes. Remove and drop into the ice water to stop the cooking process.

Using your hands, squeeze as much water from the spinach as you can. Then, place the spinach in a clean kitchen towel and wring it out to remove all excess liquid. Once the spinach is as dry as you can get it, pulse it in a food processor to finely chop it.

In a large bowl, combine the strained ricotta and spinach, parmesan, yolks, egg, salt, pepper and nutmeg. Gently incorporate the flour, being careful not to over mix. Using a small ice cream scoop, or two spoons, form the mixture into 1 ½ ounce (43 g) dumplings. Carefully drop the dumplings into boiling water and cook for 8 to 10 minutes. Remove from water and serve.

GARLIC CHIPS

These chips are a great garnish for any dish, especially the Braised Pork Shanks (page 76). They immediately add texture and flavor to whatever you're serving. Personally, I just love snacking on them!

YIELD: 1 CUP (60 G)

20 garlic cloves, peeled

3 cups (710 ml) milk

1 tsp salt

3 cups (710 ml) canola oil

Slice the garlic cloves as thinly as possible. I highly recommend using a mandoline.

Heat the milk and salt in a small saucepan until simmering. Poach the garlic in the simmering milk for 5 minutes. Strain the milk and dry the garlic on paper towels.

Heat the canola oil in a medium saucepan until it reaches 300°F (149°C). Gently place the garlic into the hot oil and fry until golden brown. Place the chips on paper towel to strain the grease.

WHITE CHOCOLATE POUND CAKE WITH CANDIED GRAPEFRUIT AND GRAPEFRUIT CARAMEL

This cake is rich and dense—perfect for cold weather. Serving it alongside the Candied Grapefruit (page 83) and Grapefruit Caramel (page 83) brightens up the citrus flavors, which make a nice contrast to the sweetness of the white chocolate.

YIELD: 8 TO 10 SERVINGS

6 oz (170 g) white chocolate chips

½ cup (118 g) heavy cream

4 eggs, separated

1 cup (230 g) or 2 sticks butter, softened

2 cups (383 g) sugar

1 cup (237 ml) buttermilk

1 tsp vanilla extract

1 ½ cups (187 g) flour

1 tsp baking soda

¼ tsp salt

Candied Grapefruit (page 83)
Grapefruit Caramel (page 83)

Preheat the oven to 350°F (177°C).

Using a double boiler, melt the white chocolate and heavy cream. Set aside.

Whip the egg whites in a KitchenAid® stand mixer with the whisk attachment until stiff. Set aside.

Still using the stand mixer, but with the paddle attachment, cream the butter and sugar. Add the egg yolks, melted chocolate, buttermilk and vanilla extract until combined.

In a separate bowl, combine the flour, baking soda and salt. Add it to the wet mixture, in batches, until fully incorporated. Stir in about a third of the egg whites to lighten the batter, and then fold in the rest.

Add the batter into a greased and floured 9 x 5 inch (23 x 13 cm) loaf pan. Bake for 1 hour in the preheated oven, or until a toothpick comes out clean when inserted in the cake. Allow to cool on a rack for 15 minutes before inverting the pan to remove the cake.

Serve with Candied Grapefruit and Grapefruit Caramel.

Stored covered at room temperature for up to 2 days.

CANDIED GRAPEFRUIT

These are great little treats that can accompany any kind of dessert, or be served alongside coffee at the end of a meal. Blanching them several times helps to remove the bitterness from the rinds, and the end result is a sweet grapefruit candy without any tartness.

YIELD: 8 TO 10 SERVINGS

3 grapefruits

¾ cup (177 ml) water, plus more

10 cups (1.9 kg) sugar

Wash each grapefruit and cut in half. Juice the fruit and discard. Using a paring knife, remove what's left from the inside of the grapefruit and discard. Slice the rind into ¼ inch (6 mm) slices and place in a small saucepan. Cover the rinds with water and bring to a boil. When the water begins boiling, remove from heat and strain out the water. Repeat this blanching process 4 more times.

When the rinds are all blanched, place 7 cups (1.3 kg) of sugar and ¾ cups (177 ml) of water into a saucepan and stir until the sugar is moistened. Add the grapefruit rinds and bring to a boil. Cook for 40 minutes, or until the rinds become translucent. Remove from heat and drain the syrup, making sure to save it. Allow the rinds to cool for about 4 to 5 minutes.

Place the remaining 3 cups (575 g) of sugar into a bowl and toss the rinds to thoroughly coat. Allow the rinds to sit on a cooling rack for about an hour before eating.

GRAPEFRUIT CARAMEL

This caramel is essentially the dessert version of sweet and sour sauce. It's fantastic!
The acidity in the grapefruit keeps any dessert you serve it with from being too sweet.
Drizzle it over cakes or ice cream and call it a perfect end to the day.

YIELD: 6 SERVINGS

4 cups (946 ml) fresh grapefruit juice

8 tbsp (115 g) butter

2 cups (383 g) sugar

1 cup (237 ml) heavy cream

1 tsp salt

In a medium saucepan over high heat, reduce the grapefruit juice to ½ cup (118 ml), about 15 minutes, and strain. Set aside. Meanwhile, heat the butter and sugar in a heavy saucepan over medium heat until lightly caramelized, 8 to 10 minutes. Make sure to stir frequently so the sugar browns evenly. Carefully add the reduced grapefruit juice and heavy cream. Be careful as the caramel will bubble up. Don't worry if the sugar hardens; just simmer and continue stirring until the sugar dissolves and the caramel is smooth, about 5 minutes. Stir in the salt and allow the caramel to cool before using.

TOMATO BISQUE WITH FRESH MOZZARELLA AND BASIL

Nothing is cozier on a cold winter's day than a comforting bowl of soup.
This creamy bisque is extremely easy to whip up and it keeps in the fridge for a few days, so you're
guaranteed a good meal at any time. I like to serve it with grilled cheese or fresh mozzarella,
or you can simply garnish it with parmesan or basil. This recipe is quite versatile, so feel free
to experiment with different spices and herbs to make it your own.

YIELD: 6 TO 8 SERVINGS

8 tbsp (115 g) butter

2 onions, sliced

¼ cup (38 g) chopped garlic

32 oz (908 g) canned tomato

1 tsp (2 g) chili flakes

4 cups (945 ml) heavy cream

Salt and pepper to taste

Fresh mozzarella

Basil, chopped

Add the butter to a large pot over medium heat. Sweat the onions and garlic until translucent and they begin to caramelize, about 8 to 10 minutes. Add the canned tomatoes, chili flakes and heavy cream and cook for 20 minutes. Remove from heat and puree, in batches, in a blender. Season with salt and pepper to taste. Garnish with the mozzarella and basil.

Once cooled, store in an airtight container in the refrigerator for up to 5 days.

Note

If possible, use San Marzano canned tomatoes; I think they have the best flavor.

ENDIVE SALAD WITH GRAPEFRUIT, ROASTED PISTACHIOS, ROASTED BEETS AND PISTACHIO PESTO

This winter salad is lovely and colorful, even when the weather is everything but. Hearty, bitter endives are tossed with grapefruit, bright red beets and green pistachios for a tasty, crunchy and fresh meal. Luckily, grapefruits are at their peak during winter, so they truly shine in this salad.

YIELD: 4 SERVINGS

1 ½ lbs (680 g) white endive

2 grapefruits, segmented

½ cup (85 g) Roasted Pistachios (page 88)

2 cups (459 g) Roasted Beets (page 89), cut into chunks

¼ cup (59 ml) olive oil

1 tbsp (15 g) sea salt

1 cup (116 g) Pistachio Pesto (page 90)

Remove the leaves from the endives and cut into large pieces. Toss with the grapefruit segments, pistachios, beets, olive oil and sea salt.

Spoon the pesto onto your serving plate to make a bed for the salad. Add some of the tossed salad onto the pesto. Serve immediately.

Note

The grapefruit is acidic enough that the salad doesn't really need a dressing, but if you want a little more, I recommend using Champagne vinegar. Endives can be white or red; although either color can work for this salad, I prefer the white for a stunning color contrast.

ROASTED PISTACHIOS

These pistachios are a great garnish to any salad, but they're also delicious as a snack. Roasting the pistachios with honey gives them a touch of sweetness that brings out their natural, buttery flavor.

YIELD: 1 ½ CUPS (256 G)

2 tbsp (30 ml) honey

2 tsp (10 g) salt

2 tbsp (30 ml) olive oil

1 ½ cups (256 g) pistachios

Preheat the oven to 325°F (163°C).

Whisk together the honey, salt and olive oil. Toss the raw pistachios with the honey mixture and pour onto a parchment-lined cookie sheet. Toast in the oven until the honey is bubbling and you can smell the nuts roasting, about 10 to 15 minutes. Remove from the oven and cool completely before using.

Once cooled, roughly chop the pistachios with a knife. Pistachios can be stored in an airtight container at room temperature for up to a month.

ROASTED BEETS

This is my favorite way of cooking beets. The Champagne vinegar gives them a light pickle flavor and their bright red color is lovely. I like adding them to salads for a heartier meal.

YIELD: 6 SERVINGS

2 lbs (907 g) red beets

3 cups (710 ml) Champagne vinegar

2 cups (473 ml) water

2 tbsp (30 g) salt

Preheat the oven to 400°F (205°C).

Combine the beets, vinegar, water and salt in a roasting pan and put in the oven. Roast for 1 ½ hours.

To check if they're done, stick a toothpick in them. If the toothpick goes in smoothly, they're done. If there's any resistance, return beets to the oven and cook for another 30 minutes.

Remove the beets from the liquid and using a towel, rub off the skins and discard. Cut them anyway you'd like. Beets will keep in an airtight container in the refrigerator for 3 to 4 days.

Note

You can use beets of any color for this dish.

PISTACHIO PESTO

This recipe is a great alternative to traditional pesto, and it's also healthier than the cheesy pesto variety. The pistachio adds a buttery nuttiness that goes well with bitter greens and meats, and the spinach gives the pesto its bright green color. Use it just as you'd use traditional pesto.

YIELD: 6 TO 8 SERVINGS

1 cup (170 g) pistachios

3 garlic cloves, peeled

15 basil leaves

2 cups (80 g) baby spinach

½ cup (118 ml) olive oil

1 ½ tsp (8 g) salt

Preheat the oven to 350°F (177°C).

Toast the pistachios on a cookie sheet in the oven for 7 minutes. Allow to cool.

Add the toasted pistachios and garlic to a food processor and pulse until coarse. Add the basil, spinach, olive oil and salt and pulse until incorporated.

Store in an airtight container in the refrigerator for up to 3 days.

Note

Be careful not to overwork the pistachios in the food processor. They'll turn to pistachio butter if pulsed too long. Don't skip toasting the pistachios! It helps them release their natural oils and flavors.

CLAMS AND "SPAGHETTI" WITH SPICY GARLIC CROUTONS

Clams and spaghetti is a classic New England dish that you'll see on menus everywhere,
and this is my take on it. Spaghetti squash is one of my favorite vegetables.
Its insides resemble strands of spaghetti, minus all of the extra carbs.
These croutons add the perfect spicy, buttery crunch.

YIELD: 4 SERVINGS

2 lbs (907 g) spaghetti squash

4 tsp (20 g) salt

24 little neck clams

4 tbsp (57 g) butter

3 tbsp (28 g) sliced garlic

¼ cup (33 g) sliced shallots

½ cup (118 ml) white wine

½ cup (80 g) diced tomatoes

1 tbsp (3 g) fresh oregano leaves

½ tsp pepper

2 tbsp (30 ml) lemon juice

SPICY GARLIC CROUTONS

3 cups (450 g) day-old bread, cut
into ½–inch (13-mm) cubes

3 tbsp (43 g) butter, melted

2 tbsp (30 ml) olive oil

2 tsp (1 g) chili flakes

4 tbsp (38 g) minced garlic

1 tbsp (15 g) salt

1 tsp pepper

1 tbsp (2 g) dried oregano

Preheat the oven to 400°F (205°C).

Cut the spaghetti squash in half and season with 2 teaspoons (10 g) of salt. Place, cut side down, on a baking sheet and roast in the preheated oven for 20 to 25 minutes, or until tender. Remove from the oven and allow to cool.

Using a fork, separate the squash's inner flesh from its skin. It should resemble spaghetti. Set aside.

Wash the clams under cold water. Heat a sauté pan on medium-high heat and add the butter, garlic and shallots. Sauté until tender, about 5 minutes. Add the washed clams to the pan and deglaze with the white wine. Cook, covered, until the clams begin to open, about 4 to 6 minutes. Add the spaghetti squash, diced tomatoes, oregano, remaining salt, pepper and lemon juice. Continue cooking until the clams are fully open, about 4 to 6 minutes. Remove from heat and garnish with the Spicy Garlic Croutons.

To make the croutons, preheat the oven to 350°F (177°C).

Combine all of the ingredients in a large bowl, tossing well to completely coat the bread. Transfer to a cookie sheet and toast in the oven for 10 minutes. Stir bread and toast for another 10 minutes, until the bread is crispy. Remove from the oven and allow to cool to room temperature.

SPICY CHICKEN STEW WITH CORNMEAL DUMPLINGS

This recipe reminds me of my grandmother. Many winters ago, she served me
a heaping bowl of chicken and dumplings on a cold, snowy day and it completely blew me away.
This recipe is everything you want on a cold winter's day: hearty, warming and stocked with carbs.

YIELD: 10 TO 12 SERVINGS

2 cups (250 g) flour

3 tbsp (45 g) salt

1 tbsp (15 g) pepper

2 tbsp (15 g) Cajun seasoning

5 lbs (2.3 kg) chicken thighs, diced

1 cup (237 ml) canola oil

½ lb (227 g) butter

4 cups (610 g) diced carrots

6 cups (909 g) diced onions

3 cups (454 g) diced celery

6 cups (1 kg) diced sweet potatoes

8 quarts (7.6 l) Chicken Stock
(page 197)

2 tbsp (3 g) dried oregano

2 oz (57 g) fresh rosemary sprigs,
secured with twine for easy removal

CORNMEAL DUMPLINGS

1 ⅓ cups (167 g) flour

⅔ cup (114 g) cornmeal

2 tsp (8 g) brown sugar

2 tsp (8 g) baking powder

2 tbsp (29 g) butter, melted

1 cup (237 ml) milk

1 tbsp (15 g) salt

½ tsp cayenne

Preheat the oven to 350°F (177°C)

In a medium bowl, combine the flour, salt, pepper and Cajun seasoning. Dredge the diced chicken in the flour mixture. Heat the canola oil and butter in a rondeau, or a wide and shallow pan. Add the floured chicken and cook until lightly browned, about 8 to 10 minutes. Add any leftover flour to the pan and cook for 5 more minutes. Add the carrots, onions, celery and sweet potatoes and cook for 5 minutes. Add the stock, oregano and rosemary and simmer until the chicken is tender and fully cooked, about 25 to 30 minutes. Once the chicken is cooked, remove the rosemary and set aside.

Mix all the dumpling ingredients together in a medium bowl. Dumpling batter should look like very thick pancake batter.

Drop spoonfuls of the dumpling dough into the stew. Cover and cook until the dumplings double in size and are fully cooked, about 8 minutes.

BRAISED SHORT RIBS WITH PARSNIP PUREE AND SQUASH SLAW

This meaty, rich and spiced braise is the perfect Sunday supper recipe, especially on a cold night. It does take time and effort to make, but the end result is definitely worth it. If you miraculously have leftovers, the ribs are delicious in a sandwich the next day (just remember to remove any bones).

YIELD: 8 TO 10 SERVINGS

¼ cup (59 ml) canola oil

2 tbsp (30 g) salt

1 tbsp (15 g) pepper

5 lbs (2.3 kg) short ribs

2 onions, sliced

¼ cup (40 g) garlic cloves

1 jalapeño

2 oz (57 g) ginger, peeled and sliced

1 cup (237 ml) red wine

8 oz (227 g) canned tomatoes

10 cups (2.4 l) Chicken Stock (page 197)

1 cinnamon stick

4 allspice berries

1 tbsp (8 g) peppercorns

1 bay leaf

3 sprigs of rosemary

4 sprigs of thyme

¼ cup (60 ml) maple syrup

SERVE WITH

Parsnip Puree (page 98)

Squash Slaw (page 98)

Preheat the oven to 325°F (163°C).

Heat the canola oil in a rondeau, or wide and shallow pan, over high heat.

Season the short ribs with salt and pepper. Place in the hot pan and sear on all sides. Transfer to a deep roasting pan.

In the same pan used to sear the short ribs, caramelize the onions, cooking for 8 minutes. Add the garlic, jalapeño and ginger and cook until tender, about 8 to 10 minutes. Add the wine and tomatoes and cook until almost completely reduced, about 15 minutes. Add the stock, herbs, spices and maple syrup and cook for another 20 minutes.

Cover the seared short ribs with the braising liquid and cover with foil. Cook for 4 hours in the oven. The short ribs are done when they're fork-tender and almost falling off the bone.

When the short ribs are done, allow to cool to room temperature in the braising liquid. Once cooled, remove the short ribs from the liquid and set aside. Strain the braising liquid and reduce it in a stockpot over high heat. The sauce is done once it's reduced by ¾ of its original amount. Add the short ribs back into the reduced sauce and bring back up to temperature. Serve right away with a side of Parsnip Puree and Squash Slaw.

Note

I prefer to use boneless short ribs for this recipe, but they can be hard to find. Short ribs with the bones are perfectly fine and you'll actually get some extra flavor from the bones.

PARSNIP PUREE

Move over mashed potatoes! This recipe celebrates the delicious parsnip. Parsnips are at
their peak during wintertime and they just so happen to pair wonderfully with hearty, winter foods
like the Braised Short Ribs (page 97). In this recipe, the sweet and earthy root vegetable
is pureed with onions to bring out its natural sweetness.

YIELD: 4 TO 6 SERVINGS

2 ½ lbs (1.13 kg) parsnips

1 onion, sliced

2 tbsp (29 g) butter

1 tbsp (15 g) salt

3 cups (700 ml) milk

Peel and roughly chop parsnips.

In a saucepan, sweat the onions in the butter and salt until tender, about 5 to
8 minutes. Add the parsnips and milk. Cover and cook until the parsnips are
tender, about 15 minutes. Remove the parsnips and onions from the milk and
puree in a blender until smooth. Use the milk as needed to thin it out to your
desired consistency.

SQUASH SLAW

Slaw isn't just for summer barbecues. This winter-appropriate slaw has bright flavors, while still being
hearty enough for a chilly winter's day. It's much lighter than mayonnaise-based slaws and, I think,
much tastier, too. If you've never had raw butternut squash, don't fret! It's sweet and crunchy
and its beautiful orange color is a sight for sore eyes.

YIELD: 10 TO 12 SERVINGS

1 cup (237 ml) cider vinegar

½ cup (120 ml) maple syrup

¼ cup (63 g) whole grain mustard

2 tbsp (5 g) picked thyme

2 tsp (10 g) + 2 tbsp (30 g) salt

1 cup (237 ml) canola oil

2 lbs (907 g) butternut squash,
seeds removed, peeled and grated

1 head of green cabbage, julienned

6 scallions, julienned

1 red onion, julienned

Add the vinegar, maple syrup, mustard, thyme and 2 teaspoons (10 g) of
salt to a blender. Blend while slowly drizzling in the canola oil to emulsify
completely. Set aside.

Mix the grated squash, cabbage, scallions, red onions and 2 tablespoons
(30 g) of salt together. Allow to sit for 5 minutes. Drain any excess liquid and
toss with the dressing.

Slaw can be stored in the refrigerator for up to a week in an airtight container.
If it seems too soupy, just drain off some of the liquid before eating.

CHOCOLATE MINT BREAD PUDDING

This gooey, rich bread pudding is great for a holiday gathering. It's delicious, impressive and quite easy to make. As the bread pudding bakes, the chocolate chips create wonderful pockets of molten chocolate. It's soft and gooey inside, but the top has some crunch and texture to it.

YIELD: 8 TO 10 SERVINGS

8 cups (650 g) brioche bread, cubed

6 eggs

2 ½ cups (592 ml) cream

2 tsp (10 ml) peppermint extract

½ cup (96 g) sugar

2 cups (360 g) milk chocolate chips

Preheat the oven to 325°F (163°C).

Put the brioche cubes into a glass baking dish.

In a large bowl, whisk together the eggs, cream, peppermint extract and sugar until well combined. Pour the mixture over the bread and stir in the chocolate chips. Let the bread soak up the pudding mixture for 10 minutes.

Bake in the preheated oven for 1 hour. Serve warm with chocolate sauce and vanilla ice cream.

You can make this recipe ahead by preparing it up until the point where it goes in the oven. Keep the unbaked pudding in the refrigerator until ready to bake. Remember to add an extra 5 minutes to your baking time.

Note

A plain chocolate bread pudding can be made by substituting vanilla extract for the peppermint extract. I recommend using any kind of sweet bread in this recipe, but white bread will work just as well.

Spring

Spring is traditionally all about hope. Finally, the days begin to get longer and the temperatures slowly rise above freezing. New life is popping up all around, and it's hard not to feel refreshed and hopeful for the upcoming season. Everything is green again, and so is this chapter. With spring come all the green foods we can get our hands on. These menus are all about celebrating fresh meals while slowly shedding our winter selves, until the cold arrives again.

Spring's produce is plentiful. In these recipes you'll find the freshest flavors of spring: English peas, fava beans, green garlic, baby vegetables, fiddleheads, nettles, new potatoes, ramps, rhubarb, lamb, and fortunately for us, the list goes on and on.

Dust off your outdoor chairs and have yourself an al fresco dinner, or invite loved ones for a spring-appropriate brunch. If the weather won't budge, cozy up with a fresh but surely hearty dinner that's a match for chilly spring nights. Regardless, get ready to lighten up!

CRAB CAKES WITH BACON EMULSION AND JICAMA

The flavors in this dish come together in perfect, delicious harmony. Whether you're having a nice springtime lunch with friends or a fancy dinner party, this recipe is sure to be a hit.

YIELD: 8 SERVINGS

1 cup (40 g) baby arugula

1 ½ cups (181 g) jicama, julienned

2 tsp (10 ml) lemon juice

1 ½ tsp (8 ml) olive oil

1 tsp sea salt

SERVE WITH

¾ cup (177 ml) Bacon Emulsion (page 107)

8 Crab Cakes (page 106)

In a small bowl, mix together the arugula, jicama, lemon juice, olive oil and sea salt.

Place a dollop of the Bacon Emulsion onto each crab cake. Top each crab cake with some of the salad. Serve immediately.

CRAB CAKES

These crab cakes are light and vibrant in flavor. The addition of green garlic and sorrel in this recipe really brightens it up, making it the ultimate celebration that winter is over! Sorrel is an herb with a citrusy flavor; it's beautifully delicate and green.

YIELD: 8 TO 10 SERVINGS

1 ½ lbs (680 g) jumbo lump crab meat

5 cups (296 g) focaccia, diced small

½ cup (75 g) red onion, diced small

¼ cup (12 g) scallion chiffonade

3 tbsp (30 g) green garlic, thinly sliced

1 tbsp (7 g) ground mustard

2 tsp (5 g) Old Bay® seasoning

1 lemon, zested

3 eggs

2 tbsp (5 g) sorrel chiffonade

2 tsp (10 g) salt

½ tsp pepper

½ tsp paprika

1 ½ cups (149 g) flour

1 ½ cups (344 g) beaten eggs

1 ½ cups (181 g) Panko breadcrumbs

Canola oil, for frying the crab cakes

Drain the crab meat in a strainer, making sure to push out any excess moisture. Mix the crab meat with all of the ingredients except the flour, eggs and Panko. Portion out 3-ounce (85-g) balls from the crab meat mix and gently flatten to create a disk-like shape.

Bread the cakes by dipping them first in flour, then in the beaten eggs, and lastly in the Panko.

Heat a sauté pan on medium heat and coat the bottom with canola oil. Sear crab cakes on both sides until crispy. Serve immediately.

Store any unused or leftover crab cakes in the refrigerator for up to 2 days. It's best to just cook everything at once and store any leftover cakes in the fridge.

Note

I like using focaccia for this recipe, but any dense Italian bread will work just as well.

BACON EMULSION

This is essentially bacon mayonnaise. The ingredients are emulsified together to create silky, bacon-flavored goodness. I've been known to dip carrots and broccoli in it as a snack, but if you're an extreme bacon-lover, try it on a BLT sandwich.

YIELD: 8 TO 10 SERVINGS

½ cup (118 g) bacon fat

3 oz (85 g) cooked bacon

3 tbsp (47 g) Dijon mustard

2 oz (57 g) shallots, diced

3 garlic cloves

¼ cup (59 ml) lemon juice

5 egg yolks

2 cups (437 ml) canola oil

2 ½ tsp (13 g) salt

Warm the bacon fat only to the moment when it becomes a pourable liquid.

In a food processor, puree the cooked bacon, mustard, shallots, garlic, lemon juice and egg yolks. Slowly drizzle the bacon fat while the food processor is still running. Drizzle in the canola oil until completely emulsified. Season with salt.

Store in an airtight container in the refrigerator for up to 4 days.

RED LEAF LETTUCE WITH ASPARAGUS, RHUBARB AND LEMON POPPY VINAIGRETTE

This salad is a gentle reintroduction of springtime flavors. The combination of raw asparagus, sour rhubarb and creamy Lemon Poppy Vinaigrette (page 111) is a refreshing change of pace from the heartiness of winter dishes. I love the rawness, crunch and sourness of this salad.

YIELD: 4 SERVINGS

1 head red leaf lettuce

½ lb (227 g) fresh asparagus

1 stalk fresh rhubarb

½ cup (115 g) julienned radish

1 tbsp (15 g) sea salt

SERVE WITH

¾ cup (177 ml) Lemon Poppy Vinaigrette (page 111)

Slice the lettuce into large ribbons and wash under cold water. Allow to dry on paper towels.

Using a vegetable peeler, peel ribbons off the asparagus. Set aside. Peel ribbons off the rhubarb and place them in ice water so they'll curl up beautifully.

In a large bowl, gently mix all of the ingredients together. Serve right away.

Note

Raw rhubarb can be very sour and fibrous. Using a vegetable peeler to peel it into ribbons ensures that it won't overpower the rest of the ingredients.

LEMON POPPY VINAIGRETTE

This citrusy dressing is sure to brighten up any salad, especially the Red Leaf Lettuce with Asparagus and Rhubarb (page 108). The poppy seeds give it a nice texture, not to mention a beautiful speckled look. This vinaigrette manages to be refreshing yet creamy, the perfect balance for spring meals.

YIELD: 6 TO 8 SERVINGS

½ cup (118 ml) fresh lemon juice

½ cup (118 ml) buttermilk

½ cup (60 g) sour cream

2 lemons, zested

¼ cup (50 g) chopped shallots

2 tbsp (6 g) chopped thyme

2 tbsp (17 g) poppy seeds

½ cup (118 ml) honey

2 ½ tsp (13 g) salt

1 cup (237 ml) olive oil

Whisk together the lemon juice, buttermilk, sour cream, lemon zest, shallots, thyme, poppy seeds, honey and salt. Slowly drizzle in the olive oil, whisking to fully incorporate. Keep refrigerated.

If stored in an airtight container in the refrigerator, vinaigrette will last for up to a week.

SEARED SCALLOPS WITH ORANGE BRAISED CARROTS, SWEET PEA PUREE AND PEA TENDRILS

Scallops are sweet and taste of the ocean, in the best way possible. I like to baste them in butter, or some kind of fat to add a level of richness to them. Serve them with Orange Braised Carrots (page 115) and Sweet Pea Puree (page 116), on a salad or even just by themselves. Bacon is always a good option, and these scallops pair wonderfully with it.

YIELD: 4 SERVINGS

16 fresh U/10* sea scallops

4 tbsp (59 ml) canola oil

Salt, to taste

4 tbsp (57 g) butter

SERVE WITH

Orange Braised Carrots (page 115)

Sweet Pea Puree (page 116)

Dry the scallops with a paper towel. Drying the scallops well ensures that they'll be more evenly browned and that there's less of a chance of them sticking to the pan.

Heat a sauté pan or cast iron pan over high heat and add the canola oil. Sprinkle salt on the scallops and sear immediately. The longer the salt stays on the scallops before searing, the more moisture it'll extract. Once the scallops are in the hot pan, don't move them! Each time you move them around, the cooking process is interrupted.

When some color begins to form on the bottom of the scallops, turn the heat down to medium-low and allow them to cook for 5 more minutes. Flip the scallops and add the butter to the pan. Cook for another 3 minutes. Using a spoon, baste the scallops with butter. Transfer to paper towels to drain some of the fat. Serve immediately with the braised carrots and Sweet Pea Puree.

Note

*"U/10" refers to the number of scallops in a pound. The same type of sizing is used with shrimp.

ORANGE BRAISED CARROTS

This recipe has bright floral flavors that are perfect for a spring side dish. The pink peppercorns give it its floral flavor, so don't skip them. Orange pairs well with the carrots, bringing out their sweetness and balancing it with some acidity.

YIELD: 8 SERVINGS

2 ½ lbs (1 kg) carrots

½ lb (227 g) butter

3 oz (85 g) shallots, sliced

2 tsp (6 g) pink peppercorns, ground

1 tsp turmeric

2 cups (473 ml) orange juice

1 ½ tbsp (23 g) salt

Peel and cut carrots into desired shapes.

In a rondeau, or a wide and shallow pan, add the butter, shallots, peppercorns and turmeric and cook until the shallots are soft, about 6 minutes. Add the carrots, orange juice and salt and cook until the carrots are slightly tender but still have some bite to them, about 10 to 12 minutes. Serve immediately.

Note

Avoid using store-bought orange juice in this recipe and opt for fresh-squeezed. I recommend using baby carrots, if you can find them.

SWEET PEA PUREE

This recipe tastes and looks like spring. It's fresh, vibrant and has a bright green color. I can't think of anything more spring-like than peas, mint and basil. Serve this as a side or try mixing in ½ pound (227 g) of ricotta cheese to make a delicious spread or dip.

YIELD: 8 SERVINGS

2 lbs (907 g) peas

3 cups (121 g) pea tendrils

¼ cup (10 g) mint leaves

¼ cup (10 g) basil leaves

4 tbsp (57 g) butter

¼ cup (33 g) sliced shallots

⅛ cup (20 g) sliced garlic

1 lemon, zested and juiced

2 ½ tsp (13 g) salt

½ tsp pepper

Bring a large pot of water to a boil. Blanch the peas until tender and shock them in ice water to stop the cooking process. Blanch and shock the pea tendrils, mint and basil. Set aside.

Heat the butter in a sauté pan over medium heat until it begins to bubble. Sauté the shallots and garlic until they begin to caramelize, about 5 minutes. Remove from the heat and set aside.

Add the peas, herbs, shallots, garlic, lemon juice, zest, salt and pepper to a blender and blend until smooth. If the puree is too dry, add water to the mixture a little bit at a time until smooth.

Garnish with pea tendrils and serve.

RACK OF LAMB WITH OLIVE OIL CRUSHED POTATOES AND MINTED FAVA BEANS

This recipe is easy breezy and quite impressive to serve at dinner parties. The mustard gives it a good bite and it actually works quite nicely with the natural flavors of the lamb.

YIELD: 4 SERVINGS

½ cup (60 g) Panko bread crumbs

¼ cup (63 g) Dijon mustard

2 racks of lamb 1 ½ to 2 lbs (680 to 907 g)

1 tbsp (15 g) salt

1 tsp pepper

SERVE WITH

Olive Oil Crushed Potatoes (page 120)

Minted Fava Beans (page 120)

Preheat the oven to 400°F (205°C).

Pour the bread crumbs on a plate. Set aside.

Using a pastry brush, smear the mustard on the meaty part of the lamb. Season the meat with salt and pepper. Press the seasoned lamb onto the bread crumbs to coat it thoroughly. Bake in the preheated oven until the internal temperature of the lamb reads 125°F (52°C) on a meat thermometer, about 15 minutes.

Remove from the oven and allow to rest for 4 to 5 minutes. Serve immediately with potatoes and fava beans.

Note

If possible, buy "frenched" lamb racks. These are the racks where the bones are clean up to the point where the loin begins.

OLIVE OIL CRUSHED POTATOES

This recipe is simple and so versatile. Brunch it up by serving the potatoes alongside crispy fried eggs or for dinner with a heartier protein. These potatoes demonstrate that you don't need a ton of ingredients to make something taste incredible.

YIELD: 6 SERVINGS

3 lbs (1.4 kg) new potatoes

½ cup (118 ml) olive oil

¼ cup (59 ml) lemon juice

2 tbsp (5 g) chopped parsley

1 ½ tbsp (23 g) salt

2 tsp (10 g) pepper

Place the potatoes in a large pot and cover them with cold water. Bring to a boil and cook until they're soft, about 20 to 25 minutes. Strain and allow them to cool on a wire rack. Once cooled, lay the potatoes on a cutting board and gently crush them with the palm of your hand.

Heat a sauté pan over medium heat and add the olive oil. Add the crushed potatoes to the pan and cook until hot and crispy, about 6 to 8 minutes. Add the lemon juice, parsley, salt and pepper and incorporate them into the potatoes by lightly crushing them with a fork. Be careful not to overwork them or they'll get gummy. Serve immediately.

MINTED FAVA BEANS

If you're not a fan of fava beans, I'm willing to bet that you've never had them fresh at the height of their season. While using fresh beans does take a little more prep time, their flavor is far superior to any of the precleaned beans you'll find.

YIELD: 4 TO 6 SERVINGS

5 lbs (2.3 kg) fresh fava beans

3 tbsp (43 g) butter

2 tsp (10 g) salt

1 ½ tbsp (4 g) fresh mint, cut into chiffonade

Shuck the fava beans out of their pods. Then, bring a pot of water to a boil, and fill a large bowl up with ice water. Blanch the beans in the boiling water for 4 minutes, and immediately shock them in the ice water.

Remove the outer, waxy layer of the beans by cutting off a thin layer of the top of the bean, and then squeezing the inner bean into a separate bowl. Once peeled, blanch the beans in the boiling water for 3 minutes and immediately shock them in the ice water.

Heat a sauté pan over medium heat and cook the butter until it begins to bubble. Add the blanched fava beans and gently press them with a fork to break them apart. Remove the pan from the heat and season them with the salt and mint. Serve immediately.

VANILLA CUSTARD WITH POACHED RHUBARB AND FRESH STRAWBERRIES

This custard is a blank canvas for a variety of toppings, from fruits to chocolate. It's rich and simple, but also delicious just on its own. I love the simplicity of this dish and recommend you use it as a vehicle for the freshest fruit of the season, such as Poached Rhubarb (page 124).

YIELD: 8 SERVINGS

15 fresh strawberries

3 ½ cups (828 ml) milk

2 tbsp (30 ml) vanilla extract

8 egg yolks

¾ cup (144 g) sugar

½ tsp salt

SERVE WITH
Poached Rhubarb (page 124)

Wash and clean strawberries. Cut in half or quarters, depending on their size. Set aside.

Heat the milk and vanilla in a saucepan until the mixture begins to simmer. Remove from heat.

Using a KitchenAid® stand mixer with the whisk attachment, beat the egg yolks and sugar until the mixture looks pale yellow in color, about 5 to 6 minutes. While the mixer is on low speed, slowly drizzle in the warm milk and vanilla mixture. Be careful not to pour too much at once or you'll end up with scrambled eggs. Once fully incorporated, add the salt and place the mixture back into the saucepan over medium heat. Stir constantly. Cook until it coats the back of a spoon and it's starting to thicken. Remove from heat and strain through a fine-mesh sieve. Chill in the refrigerator for 2 hours before serving.

When ready to serve, spoon 4 ounces (113 g) of custard into each serving bowl or glass. Top with 2 to 3 strawberries and spoon 2 to 3 ounces (57 to 85 g) of Poached Rhubarb over the strawberries. Serve right away.

Custard will keep in an airtight container in the refrigerator for up to 3 days.

POACHED RHUBARB

Poaching is a great way to use those slightly mushy fruits that may seem too ugly for anything else. Farmer's markets and local fruit vendors often sell their bruised fruit at a lower price, so you can still buy something that's in season but not too pricy. You could make this recipe with any spring fruit, but I like rhubarb. The sweet Riesling, sugar and vanilla help tone down the rhubarb's sourness and the thyme adds some earthy, herbal notes that make the dish a bit more complex. Enjoy it over yogurt in the morning or on Vanilla Custard (page 123) for dessert.

YIELD: 6 SERVINGS

2 ½ lbs (1 kg) rhubarb

1 bottle (750 ml) Riesling

1 ½ cups (288 g) sugar

1 vanilla bean, split

6 thyme sprigs

Preheat oven to 350°F (177°C).

Cut all the rhubarb into 3-inch (7.6-cm) pieces. Place in a glass baking dish.

In a pot over medium heat, cook the Riesling, sugar, vanilla and thyme until simmering. Pour over the rhubarb and cover with foil. Bake for 15 minutes in the preheated oven.

Remove from the oven and allow the rhubarb to cool. Strain the liquid and reserve. In a small saucepan over medium heat, cook the liquid down until it's reduced by half. Allow to cool completely and pour it over the rhubarb.

Rhubarb will keep in the refrigerator for up to a week.

SWEET PEA SOUP WITH FRESH ENGLISH PEAS AND PARMESAN CUSTARD

This light and delicate soup celebrates one of spring's best vegetables: peas! It's usually served hot, but feel free to serve it cold on warmer spring days. The fresh herbs are an essential part of this recipe: They give the soup its beautiful green color and add a certain freshness to the flavor. The onions bring out the sweetness of the peas. Frozen peas work best for the base of the soup, and they will be pureed, anyway. Fresh peas are blanched and added whole to the soup. Serve it with various tartines or add cooked bacon chunks on top for a meatier meal.

YIELD: 6 SERVINGS

1 onion, sliced

3 tbsp (43 g) butter

4 cups (606 g) frozen peas

4 cups (946 ml) Vegetable Stock (page 197)

2 tbsp (30 g) salt

1 tsp ground white pepper

¼ cup (10 g) basil leaves

2 tbsp (5 g) thyme leaves

¼ cup (10 g) parsley leaves

2 cups (303 g) fresh peas

SERVE WITH

Parmesan Custard (page 128)

In a stockpot over medium heat, sweat the onions with the butter until they're soft, about 5 minutes. Try not to get any color on them. Add the frozen peas, stock, salt and pepper and cook for about 15 minutes, until the peas are soft. Add the fresh herbs.

Remove from the heat and using a blender, puree until smooth. You might need to puree in batches as hot liquids expand.

Bring water to a boil in a small pot and blanch the fresh peas until tender, about 3 to 4 minutes. Strain and serve the peas whole in the soup.

Serve with Parmesan Custard.

PARMESAN CUSTARD

This rich and cheesy custard is one of my all-time favorite dishes. It's delicious by itself, but also great as an accompaniment to the Sweet Pea Soup (page 127), fresh asparagus, steak or chicken. You can even serve it at a brunch with poached eggs and a light salad. Feel free to change up the flavor by making it with a different kind of hard cheese. Softer cheeses won't work in this recipe since they add more moisture, and the custard simply won't set.

YIELD: 10 SERVINGS

1 cup (273 ml) milk

2 cups (473 ml) heavy cream

2 oz (57 g) thyme sprigs

2 ½ cups (450 g) grated Parmesan

2 eggs

4 egg yolks

1 tbsp (15 g) salt

1 tsp white pepper

Preheat the oven to 350°F (177°C).

In a medium saucepan over medium heat, bring the milk, cream, thyme and Parmesan to a boil. Remove from the heat and allow the mixture to steep until it reaches room temperature. Strain and discard the thyme sprigs. Set aside.

In a medium bowl, whisk the whole eggs and yolks until combined. Add the cooled milk mixture to the eggs and season with the salt and pepper.

Spray ten 8-ounce (227-g) ramekins with a cooking oil, such as PAM, and fill with 6 ounces (170 g) of custard. Place ramekins in a baking pan and add hot water to the baking pan. Water should go ¾ up the side of the ramekins. Cook for 30 to 35 minutes in the preheated oven.

Cool completely before serving.

"BUFFALO" FIDDLEHEADS WITH GORGONZOLA, BIBB LETTUCE CUPS AND BUFFALO SAUCE

This dish is fun and different. I stumbled upon these perfect fried treats while making myself a snack one day. They're a nice, spicy snack with classic Buffalo Sauce. The fiddleheads are earthy and a bit bitter, but the Gorgonzola mellows them out and adds a tangy richness.

YIELD: 4 SERVINGS

1 lb (454 g) fiddleheads

1 ½ cups (354 ml) buttermilk

1 ½ cups (187 g) flour

¼ cup (43 g) cornmeal

½ tsp paprika

1 tbsp (15 g) salt

1 tsp pepper

BUFFALO SAUCE

¾ cup (91 g) sambal

¾ cup (177 ml) hot sauce

¾ cup (177 ml) honey

¼ cup (59 ml) Champagne vinegar

1 tbsp (14 g) butter

1 cup (121 g) Gorgonzola

4 cups (946 ml) canola oil

2 Bibb lettuce leaves

Clean the fiddleheads by snipping off their ends. Prepare an ice-water bath in a large bowl. Add the buttermilk to a medium bowl. Set aside.

Bring a pot of water to a boil and blanch the fiddleheads for 2 minutes. Immediately shock them by dropping them in the ice water. Strain and add the fiddleheads to the buttermilk; soak for 15 minutes.

In another bowl, mix the flour, cornmeal, paprika, salt and pepper. Coat the buttermilk-soaked fiddleheads in the flour mixture.

To make the Buffalo Sauce in a large bowl, combine the sambal, hot sauce, honey and Champagne vinegar. Then, add the butter and gorgonzola and set aside.

Add the canola oil to a large pot and heat it to 350°F (177°C) over medium-high heat. Carefully drop the breaded fiddleheads in the oil and fry until golden brown, about 4 minutes. Using a slotted spoon or spider, carefully remove the fiddleheads from the hot oil and place in the bowl with the Buffalo Sauce. Toss to thoroughly coat. Serve in the Bibb lettuce cups.

BOSTON LETTUCE SALAD WITH PICKLED RED ONIONS, SMOKED SALMON BACON AND GREEN GODDESS DRESSING

This salad is great for spring: It's colorful and filled with vibrant flavors. The dressing is creamy, and the saltiness of the bacon and the acidity of the onions balance each other out.

YIELD: 4 SERVINGS

1 head Boston lettuce, washed and with the leaves separated

¼ cup (33 g) Pickled Red Onions (page 134)

½ cup (125 g) Smoked Salmon Bacon (page 135)

⅛ cup (30 g) Green Goddess Dressing (page 137)

1 tsp sea salt

In a large bowl, toss all ingredients together. Serve right away.

PICKLED RED ONIONS

Pickling is an extremely useful technique to learn. It helps cut down waste
and keep seasonal vegetables around for longer, especially when their season is short.
Pickling red onions gives them such a pretty pink color, and a sweet and acidic flavor that's
versatile in many dishes. Try them in salads, sandwiches and tacos.

YIELD: 5 CUPS (760 G)

5 red onions, thinly sliced

2 cups (473 ml) red wine vinegar

1 cup (237 ml) water

½ cup (96 g) sugar

2 tsp (10 g) salt

½ tsp chili flakes

3 bay leaves

2 star anises

4 thyme sprigs

Add the sliced onions to a large bowl and cover with ice. Set aside.

Add the remaining ingredients to a saucepan over medium heat and bring to a simmer. Remove from the heat and allow to cool slightly. Pour the mixture over the onions and allow to pickle in the refrigerator for 24 hours before using.

Pickled onions will last in the refrigerator for up to 2 months, if stored in an airtight container.

SMOKED SALMON BACON

This recipe doesn't actually use any bacon at all, but it still tastes like it. When salmon is baked in the oven, it dries out and gets chewy and salty like bacon. It's a delicious illusion and a fun cooking trick.

YIELD: 4 SERVINGS

1 lb (454 g) smoked salmon

Preheat the oven to 350°F (177°C).

Place the smoked salmon on a baking sheet that's lined with parchment paper. Bake for 15 minutes, until it begins to looks dry and caramelized.

GREEN GODDESS DRESSING

Homemade green goddess dressing is infinitely better than the store-bought stuff,
and it's actually quite easy to make. The buttermilk adds a richness and tanginess
that's nicely balanced with the acidity of the lemon. The addition of avocado ensures
a super creamy dressing that's perfect for salads or even as a dip.

YIELD: 6 CUPS (1.4 L)

1 avocado

3 garlic cloves

1 lemon, zested and juiced

½ cup (118 ml) buttermilk

2 egg yolks

1 ½ tbsp (23 g) salt

½ cup (118 ml) Champagne vinegar

2 cups (473 ml) canola oil

2 cups (473 ml) olive oil

½ cup (25 g) chopped chives

½ cup (20 g) chopped chervil

½ cup (20 g) chopped parsley

½ cup (25 g) chopped sorrel

½ cup (25 g) chopped basil

In a food processor, puree the avocado, garlic, lemon zest, lemon juice, buttermilk, egg yolks and salt. While the food processor is on, slowly drizzle in the Champagne vinegar until emulsified. Drizzle in the canola and olive oils until emulsified. Remove about half of the mixture and set aside in a bowl with the chives. Blend the remaining half with the rest of the herbs. Mix both mixtures together.

Store in an airtight container in the refrigerator for 4 days.

Note

If the dressing seems too thick, don't be afraid to thin it out with a bit of water.

BUCATINI WITH NETTLE PESTO AND PANCETTA

Bucatini is a thick, spaghetti-like type of pasta that has a hole running through its center. It's ideal for saucy dishes since the sauce will nestle inside the noodle. I like this dish because it's light enough to work for warm spring days while still being hearty for the chillier ones. Nettles may seem a little scary to work with at first, but as long as you handle them with gloves, you'll be fine. The nettle's spikes dissolve within 30 seconds of cooking, so you don't have to worry about eating them.

YIELD: 6 SERVINGS

½ lb (227 g) dry bucatini

NETTLE PESTO
¾ cup (94 g) pine nuts
1 ½ lbs (680 g) nettles
4 garlic cloves
1 cup (40 g) basil leaves
2 cups (85 g) baby spinach
1 lemon, zested
1 tbsp (15 g) salt
1 cup (237 ml) olive oil

1 cup (225 g) diced pancetta
2 tbsp (29 g) butter
½ cup (90 g) grated Parmesan cheese

Preheat the oven to 350°F (177°C).

Bring a large pot of water to a boil. Cook the pasta according to package instructions. Set aside.

To make the pesto, spread the pine nuts on a baking sheet and toast until golden brown, about 8 to 10 minutes. Set aside.

Wearing gloves, carefully pick the nettle leaves from their stems. Prepare an ice bath by filling a large bowl with ice water. Bring a pot of water to a boil and blanch the nettle leaves for 3 minutes, immediately shock them in the ice water. Using a strainer or cheese cloth, squeeze out the excess water from the nettles.

In a food processor, puree the nettles, pine nuts, garlic, basil, spinach, lemon zest and salt. While the food processor is running, slowly drizzle in the olive oil. Set aside.

In a sauté pan over medium heat, render the pancetta with butter until most of the fat has melted off and the pancetta begins to brown, about 5 minutes. Add the cooked pasta to the pan and toss with the pesto and grated Parmesan. Serve right away.

PAN-SEARED CHICKEN WITH MUSTARD LEMON SPAETZEL AND ROASTED BEETS

This is the ultimate crispy chicken skin recipe. Searing the skin in a pan first makes it deliciously crispy after baking in the oven, while the chicken stays moist and juicy. This dish works with practically any side, but I like serving it with Mustard Lemon Spaetzel (page 142) and Roasted Beets (page 89).

YIELD: 4 SERVINGS

2 tbsp (30 ml) canola oil

4 chicken breasts, with the skins left on

1 tsp salt

Mustard Lemon Spaetzel (page 142)

Roasted Beets (page 89)

Preheat the oven to 400°F (205°C).

Heat the canola oil in a heavy sauté pan over high heat.

Dry the chicken with paper towels and season with salt. Place the chicken, skin side down, in the sauté pan and cook until it begins to brown, 14 minutes. Flip the chicken and place the sauté pan in the preheated oven. Cook for 15 to 20 minutes, or until the chicken reaches an internal temperature of 155°F (68°C).

Remove from the oven and allow the chicken to rest, skin side up to keep it crispy, for 5 minutes.

Serve with the Mustard Lemon Spaetzel and Roasted Beets.

MUSTARD LEMON SPAETZEL

Spaetzel is a German dumpling that's similar to pasta. I love spaetzel because they soak up any sauce that they're served with, and they're extra tasty if cooked in butter until they're browned and crispy. They're hearty but light dumplings, and the mustard and lemon really brighten up their flavor.

YIELD: 6 SERVINGS

2 cups (250 g) flour

1 ½ tsp (8 g) salt

½ tsp ground nutmeg

6 large eggs

½ cup (118 ml) milk

½ cup (125 g) whole grain mustard

2 lemons, zested and juiced

In a medium bowl, whisk the flour, salt and nutmeg. In another bowl, whisk the eggs, milk, mustard, lemon zest and lemon juice.

Make a well in the flour mixture and slowly stir in the egg mixture. Once all ingredients are mixed, it should look like a thick pancake batter with a few lumps throughout. Cover the bowl with plastic wrap and allow to rest for 10 minutes at room temperature.

Prepare an ice bath by filling a large bowl with ice water. Bring a pot of water to a boil. Put all of the batter into a colander and rest over the boiling water, making sure it's not submerged. Using a rubber spatula, begin pushing the batter through the colander into the water to make noodle-shaped dumplings. Once all dumplings are in the water, cook for 3 minutes, then shock them in ice water.

Spaetzel can be made a day in advance and stored in the refrigerator until used. Simply blanch them in boiling water to reheat them.

ROASTED APRICOTS WITH YOGURT, HONEY AND ALMOND BRITTLE

This is a gorgeous, light dessert for a springtime dinner, and it can even work as a brunch main course. The apricots add sweetness to the creamy and tangy Greek yogurt, while the brittle adds a sweet crunch. Please use unsweetened Greek yogurt rather than plain yogurt for this recipe—it makes a huge difference.

YIELD: 4 SERVINGS

12 fresh apricots

2 tbsp (30 ml) honey

2 tbsp (30 ml) olive oil

2 tsp (10 g) salt

2 tbsp (5 g) mint chiffonade

4 cups (980 g) Greek yogurt

¼ cup (59 ml) honey

1 cup (170 g) Almond Brittle (page 146)

Preheat the oven to 400°F (205°C).

Cut the apricots in half and remove the pits. Place the apricots on a parchment-lined baking sheet and drizzle with honey, olive oil and salt. Roast until tender, about 15 to 20 minutes.

Toss the apricots with fresh mint. Scoop over yogurt and drizzle with honey. Garnish with the almond brittle. Serve right away.

ALMOND BRITTLE

This brittle is sweet and salty, perfect for garnishing desserts, salads or just for snacking.
Feel free to substitute a different kind of nut for the almonds.

YIELD: 2 CUPS (341 G)

1 ½ cups (288 g) sugar

¼ cup (59 ml) water

2 cups (341 g) raw almonds

1 tbsp (15 g) sea salt

In a saucepan over high heat, cook the sugar and water until the mixture turns to a caramel color. Add the almonds and continue cooking for 3 minutes, stirring the almonds so they're thoroughly coated. Carefully pour the mixture onto a greased baking sheet and sprinkle with sea salt. Allow to cool completely before breaking the brittle up into chunks.

Store brittle in an airtight container in a cool, dry place for up to a month.

Summer

While I was growing up near Cape Cod, summertime meant lots of cookouts, beach days and plenty of seafood and salty air from the ocean. I love reminiscing about those days, and these recipes are all shaped around them. When I think about summer days, what comes to mind is grilling outdoors and delicious beach food, and I especially recall fried seafood and shellfish from here in New England.

Don't worry, these recipes aren't all fried food. Summer is also about lighter foods that won't bog you down in the heat. I love meals with raw vegetables or served at room temperature around this time of year. Summer is also a lush time, with an abundance of produce. These recipes take advantage of the bounty in season: tomatoes, summer squashes, zucchini, greens, herbs, watermelon, strawberries, blueberries, peaches and, of course, corn. It's time to gather friends to have a barbecue and dine outdoors, and take advantage of the fresh, beautiful produce before fall begins!

CLAM CAKE GOUGÈRES WITH OLD BAY® AOILI

I grew up close to Cape Cod and eating clam cakes was a summer tradition. Classic clam cakes are incredibly dense and heavy, and while I have a soft spot in my heart for them, I wanted to find a way to lighten up the recipe a bit. This recipe does just that. It's the perfect marriage of the traditional clam-cake flavor without being gut-busting. I also wanted to have the option of baking or frying, depending on the occasion. Both methods are tasty, but I'm a sucker for fried foods!

YIELD: 6 SERVINGS

1 lb (450 g) chopped clams

8 tbsp (115 g) butter

1 cup (237 ml) water

1 cup (125 g) flour

1 cup (230 g) whole eggs, usually 3 eggs but crack the eggs into a measuring cup to be sure

2 tsp (5 g) Old Bay® seasoning

1 ½ tsp (8 g) salt

2 tbsp (25 g) diced shallots

2 lemons, zested

Old Bay® Aioli (page 152)

Put the chopped clams in a strainer and drain all excess liquid.

In a saucepan over medium heat, bring the butter and water to a simmer. Slowly whisk in the flour and continue cooking for 5 minutes, or until the mixture pulls away from the sides of the pan.

Remove the flour mixture from the pan and transfer to a KitchenAid® mixer with the paddle attachment. Mix on low speed for 5 minutes. Add the eggs, one at a time, until fully incorporated. This should form a soft dough.

Add the drained clams, Old Bay® seasoning, salt, shallots and lemon zest to the mixer. Continue mixing on low speed for 5 minutes.

If not using right away, dough can be stored in an airtight container in the refrigerator for up to 2 days.

TO DEEP FRY

Preheat the fryer or a pot filled halfway with canola oil to 350°F (177°C). Lower the empty basket into the hot oil, if using a fryer. Scoop the dough using a ½ ounce (14 g) scoop, or two spoons, and carefully drop it into the hot oil. Fry for 3 minutes, or until it's browned on the outside and fully cooked inside. Serve with Old Bay® Aioli.

TO BAKE

Preheat the oven to 350°F (177°C).

Using a ½ ounce (14 g) scoop, or two spoons, drop the dough onto a parchment-lined cookie sheet. Bake for 12 to 15 minutes, or until golden brown and completely cooked inside. Serve with Old Bay® Aioli.

OLD BAY® AIOLI

Old Bay® is a classic seasoning frequently used for seafood in Cape Cod, and it certainly was a staple in my family's kitchen when I was growing up. Feel free to omit the Tabasco® sauce if you don't want the aioli to be spicy, but I think it goes rather well with the Clam Cake Gougères (page 151).

YIELD: 6 TO 8 SERVINGS

6 egg yolks

¼ cup (59 ml) lemon juice

1 tbsp (16 g) Dijon mustard

2 garlic cloves

1 tbsp (15 ml) Tabasco® sauce

1 tsp salt

4 tbsp (29 g) Old Bay® seasoning

3 tbsp (44 ml) water

3 cups (710 ml) canola oil

Add the egg yolks, lemon juice, mustard, garlic, Tabasco® sauce, salt, Old Bay® seasoning and water to a food processor and pulse until smooth. While the food processor is running, drizzle in the canola oil until the mixture is thick and emulsified. If it's too thick, feel free to add a little water until it's at the consistency you desire.

Store in an airtight container in the refrigerator for up to a week.

SPINACH SALAD WITH GORGONZOLA, RED ONIONS AND BACON VINAIGRETTE

This is one of my favorite salads. It's simple, delicious and so especially hearty that no one can complain about eating salad! The Bacon Vinaigrette gives it some smoky notes, while the gorgonzola is tangy and rich. This is a great BBQ side dish.

YIELD: 4 SERVINGS

BACON VINAIGRETTE

1 lb (450 g) bacon, roughly chopped

½ cup (65 g) sliced shallots

¼ cup (38 g) sliced garlic

½ cup (125 g) whole grain mustard

¼ cup (59 ml) honey

2 tbsp (5 g) thyme leaves

1 cup (237 ml) cider vinegar

1 tbsp (15 g) salt

1 ½ tsp (6 g) pepper

1 cup (237 ml) olive oil

2 cups (473 ml) canola oil

4 cups (200 g) spinach leaves

1 cup (121 g) crumbled Gorgonzola

½ cup (65 g) thinly sliced red onions

To make the vinaigrette, render the bacon in a pan over medium heat until it gets crispy, about 8 to 10 minutes. Remove the bacon and set aside. Add the shallots and garlic to the same pan and cook until soft, about 5 minutes.

Add the bacon, bacon drippings, shallots, garlic, mustard, honey and thyme to a food processor and pulse until finely chopped. Add the vinegar, salt and pepper and pulse to combine. While the food processor is on, slowly drizzle in the olive and canola oils until combined and emulsified.

Store in an airtight container in the refrigerator for up to 2 weeks.

Toss all ingredients together in a bowl. Serve right away.

MUSSELS WITH LEMON BUTTER, PICKLED FENNEL, AND MARJORAM

This is a wonderful summer dish, especially if served outdoors on a cool night. It's light, briny, acidic and buttery. The Pickled Fennel (page 159) really makes the dish pop, and the marjoram adds an herby sweetness. I love serving it alongside crusty bread to soak up all the juices.

YIELD: 4 SERVINGS

2 tbsp (30 ml) canola oil

¼ cup (40 g) sliced garlic

¼ cup (50 g) sliced shallots

1 cup (130 g) Pickled Fennel (page 159), with the liquid strained

½ cup (118 ml) white wine

1 lb (450 g) mussels

3 tbsp (50 g) Lemon Butter (page 159)

1 ½ tbsp (4 g) fresh marjoram leaves

Heat the canola oil in a large sauté pan over high heat. Add the garlic and shallots and cook until they begin to caramelize, about 6 minutes. Add the fennel, white wine and mussels and cook for 5 minutes. Add the Lemon Butter and marjoram and cook until the mussels open completely, about 4 minutes. Serve immediately.

Note
If you can't find marjoram, substitute oregano.

LEMON BUTTER

This is an all-purpose butter. Use it on fish, chicken, beef, vegetables or whatever you like.
It's lemony and delicious for any occasion.

YIELD: ½ POUND (227 G)

½ lb (227 g) unsalted butter, at room temperature

2 lemons, zested and juiced

2 tbsp (5 g) chopped parsley

1 tsp salt

1 tsp pepper

Mix all ingredients together until thoroughly combined.

Lay out a piece of plastic wrap and put the butter on it. Shape into a log and tightly wrap.

Butter will last for up to a month in the refrigerator if wrapped well.

PICKLED FENNEL

Pickling fennel makes it acidic and savory, rather than its usual sweet self.
The use of herbs in this recipe brings out the fennel flavor even more.

YIELD: 4 CUPS (800 G)

3 fennel heads, cleaned

2 cups (473 ml) Champagne vinegar

1 cup (151 g) sliced garlic

5 bay leaves

1 ½ tbsp (13 g) pink peppercorns

1 tsp cloves

2 tsp (6 g) mustard seeds

2 tbsp (30 g) salt

½ cup (96 g) sugar

1 ½ cup (350 ml) water

1 oz (29 g) fresh oregano

Slice the fennel and place in a bowl filled with ice water. Set aside.

In a saucepan over medium heat, bring the remaining ingredients to a boil. Remove from the heat and allow to steep at room temperature for 20 minutes.

Drain the ice water from the bowl with the fennel, and cover it with 2 cups (281 g) of ice. Pour the steeped mixture over the fennel and cover. Allow to sit in the refrigerator for 24 hours prior to use.

Pickled Fennel will last in the refrigerator for up to a month, but may become more acidic as it sits.

Note

Feel free to also use the fennel greens, if you have them. They may turn brown in the pickling process but they'll only add more flavor to the dish.

GRILLED QUAIL WITH ZUCCHINI BREAD AND GREEN GARLIC BUTTER

Quail is a delicious game bird and its small size makes it perfect as an appetizer. Brining the bird helps to lightly season the meat all the way through, and also makes it extra tender. Be careful when grilling it, as the sugars in the molasses will burn more quickly than the other ingredients. As long as you keep the quail moving on the grill, you'll prevent it from charring.

This is a great appetizer for an outdoor grill dinner, especially on a cool summer night. When the Zucchini Bread is grilled, it takes on a light smokiness that's perfectly paired with the rich butter.

YIELD: 4 SERVINGS

¼ cup (20 g) sage leaves

6 thyme sprigs

½ cup (118 ml) molasses

1 tbsp (2 g) chili flakes

½ cup (121 g) + 2 tsp (10 g) salt

4 cups (946 ml) water

4 (4 to 5 oz [113 to 142 g]) boneless quails

2 tbsp (30 ml) canola oil

2 tbsp (30 ml) olive oil

4 slices Zucchini Bread (page 162), cut into ½ in- (13-mm) slices

4 tbsp (57 g) Green Garlic Butter (page 163)

In a large bowl, mix the sage, thyme, molasses, chili flakes, ½ cup (121 g) salt and water. Add the quail to the mixture and allow to brine overnight in the refrigerator.

Remove the quail from the brine and air dry in the refrigerator for 1 hour.

Heat a grill, or grill pan, over medium-high heat.

Season the quail with 2 teaspoons (10 g) of salt and rub it with the canola oil. Grill for 15 to 20 minutes, turning every couple of minutes to cook evenly. When done, the quails' internal temperature will reach 165°F (74°C).

Drizzle the olive oil over zucchini bread slices and grill until toasted on both sides. Add 1 tablespoon (14 g) of garlic butter to each slice of bread. Place the quail on top of the buttered bread and serve.

Note

If you can't find quail, feel free to substitute Cornish game hens.

ZUCCHINI BREAD

Zucchini bread is famed for being sweet, but I like to make a savory version. I recommend making this during summer months, when zucchini is at its best. If you find yourself with abundant squash, make a double batch and freeze half. If double-wrapped with plastic wrap, this bread will keep well for up to a month in the freezer. The Parmesan cheese is a tasty addition that really defines the savory aspect of the bread. Eat it alongside soup, with mashed avocado on top, or just as is!

YIELD: 8 SERVINGS

2 medium zucchinis

1 onion

1 ½ cups (187 g) flour

1 ½ tsp (6 g) baking powder

2 tsp (10 g) salt

1 tsp pepper

1 tsp paprika

1 ½ tsp (4 g) garlic powder

1 tbsp (12 g) sugar

3 eggs

2 tbsp (30 ml) milk

⅓ cup (79 ml) olive oil

½ cup (90 g) grated Parmesan cheese

2 tbsp (6 g) thyme leaves

Preheat the oven to 350°F (177°C).

Using a box grater, grate the zucchini and onion into a colander over the sink and allow to drain for 20 minutes.

In a large bowl, whisk the flour, baking powder, salt, pepper, paprika, garlic powder and sugar.

In a separate bowl, whisk the eggs, milk and olive oil. Add the grated zucchini and onion to the milk mixture and mix to combine. Slowly incorporate the wet zucchini mixture into the dry ingredients until just mixed. Add the Parmesan and thyme.

Spray a 9 x 5 inch (23 x 13 cm) loaf pan with pan spray, and add the batter into it. Bake for 45 minutes in the preheated oven, or until a toothpick comes out clean when inserted into it. Remove from the oven and allow to rest for 5 minutes before inverting the bread onto a cooling rack. Cool completely.

Bread will keep for up to 2 days as long as it's tightly wrapped in plastic wrap.

GREEN GARLIC BUTTER

Green garlic, also known as young garlic, is garlic that's pretty immature. Literally. They're pulled from the ground before they develop into the garlic we know and love, but they look like green onions with a garlicky smell. Try this butter on grilled meats, vegetables or Zucchini Bread (page 162).

YIELD: 3 CUPS (690 G)

3 cups (130 g) green garlic tops, chopped

2 tbsp (29 g) butter

1 cup (50 g) sorrel

1 lb (454 g) unsalted butter, softened

1 ½ tbsp (23 g) salt

2 tsp (10 g) pepper

2 lemons, zested

In a pan over medium heat, sauté the garlic tops in butter until soft, about 5 to 7 minutes.

Add the sautéed garlic and sorrel to a blender and puree until smooth. Combine with the softened butter and season with salt, pepper and zest. Place the butter on a sheet of plastic wrap and tightly roll into a log—you can divide the butter into two logs if it's easier. Refrigerate before using.

Butter will keep for up to a month if wrapped well in the refrigerator.

HERB-MARINATED RIB-EYE STEAK WITH CHARRED RADICCHIO AND SWEET AND SOUR CIPOLLINIS

Your first grilled meal of the summer is the unofficial start of the season, so make it a good one with this herby rib-eye recipe. The herbs freshen up the steak, while the garlic will slowly caramelize as the steak cooks and develop a deeper, slightly sweet flavor.

YIELD: 4 SERVINGS

---

10 sprigs rosemary, picked

4 sprigs oregano, picked

10 sprigs parsley, picked

8 garlic cloves

1 cup (237 ml) olive oil

3 cups (710 ml) canola oil

4 (1 lb [454 g]) rib-eye steaks

2 tbsp (30 g) salt

1 tbsp (15 g) pepper

Charred Radicchio (page 166)

Sweet and Sour Cipollinis (page 166)

In a blender, pulse the rosemary, oregano, parsley, garlic, olive oil and canola oil until smooth. Pour it over the rib-eye steaks, cover and allow to marinade in the refrigerator overnight.

Heat a grill, or grill pan, over medium heat. Season the marinated rib-eye steaks with the salt and pepper. I suggest grilling them to medium or medium-rare, about 120°F (49°C) internal temperature, or 7 minutes each side.

Serve alongside Charred Radicchio and Sweet and Sour Cipollnis.

Note

The longer the rib-eye steaks marinate, the tastier they'll be; however, don't marinate them for more than 2 days.

CHARRED RADICCHIO

Radicchio is technically a bitter green, even though it's red in color. The vinegar helps tone down the radicchio's natural bitterness, while the char flavor from grilling complements it. Serve it alongside fatty meat, as the fat will cut down the radicchio's bitterness.

YIELD: 4 SERVINGS

1 cup (237 ml) red wine vinegar

½ cup (118 ml) olive oil

1 tbsp (15 g) salt

1 tsp pepper

2 radicchio heads

Mix vinegar, olive oil, salt and pepper.

Cut the radicchio into quarters and marinate for 15 minutes in the vinegar marinade. Grill on high heat until lightly charred, about 3 minutes on each side.

SWEET AND SOUR CIPOLLINIS

Cipollinis are a smaller and sweeter type of onion. Fresh cipollini onions are relatively difficult to find, but your best bet is to scour local Italian markets for them. Some specialty grocery stores, like Whole Foods, might also carry them. The sweetness of the onions is intensified when grilled, but the balsamic vinegar adds a bit of sourness to them. They're a delicious pairing for grilled meats, or even on a cheese plate. They can be served hot or room temperature.

YIELD: 8 TO 10 SERVINGS

1 tbsp (15 ml) canola oil

2 lbs (907 g) cipollini onions, peeled

2 cups (473 ml) balsamic vinegar

1 cup (237 ml) honey

1 tbsp (15 g) salt

1 ½ tsp (8 g) pepper

Heat the canola oil in a medium saucepan over high heat. Add the cipollini onions and sear until they begin to develop some color, 6 to 8 minutes. Turn the heat down to medium. Add the vinegar, honey, salt and pepper and mix to combine. Cook until tender, about 8 minutes.

Once cooled, the onions can be refrigerated in an airtight container for up to a week.

SEARED TUNA STEAKS WITH TOMATO WATER, CORN, AVOCADO, ZUCCHINI NOODLES AND CHILIES

I love this dish because it's so fresh. All of the ingredients are essentially raw, with the exception of the tuna, which I personally prefer quite rare. There's a hint of spiciness from the red jalapeños that's perfect for all the other delicate flavors. If you'd like, you can squeeze a little lime juice over the finished dish for some extra acidity.

YIELD: 2 SERVINGS

½ cup (78 g) fresh summer corn, shucked

¼ cup (38 g) avocado, finely diced

¼ cup (38 g) zucchini, julienned

1 tbsp (13 g) red jalapeños, thinly sliced

2 Seared Tuna Steaks (page 170)

1 cup (237 ml) Tomato Water (page 171)

Make three small mounds of corn, avocado and zucchini in a large serving bowl. Sprinkle the jalapeños over the vegetables. Place the tuna in the bowl and pour the Tomato Water over it. Serve right away.

SEARED TUNA STEAKS

Tuna season in New England begins in June and goes on until September, so it's handy to have such a versatile recipe in your repertoire. The chili powder and cumin seasoning pair well with the Tomato Water, Corn, Avocado, Zucchini and Chilies (page 169) dish, but if you plan on serving it with other accompaniments, simply season with salt and pepper. Think of tuna as a blank slate for what flavor profile you want to create in a dish.

YIELD: 4 SERVINGS

2 tbsp (30 ml) canola oil

2 tbsp (30 g) salt

2 tbsp (18 g) chili powder

1 tbsp (9 g) ground cumin

4 (6 oz [170 g]) tuna steaks

Heat the canola oil in a cast iron pan over high heat.

Season the tuna steaks with salt, chili powder and cumin. Sear the tuna on each side until it's lightly browned, about 4 to 5 minutes on each side. Remove from heat and serve.

Note

I personally enjoy fresh tuna steaks served rare, but feel free to cook them to your satisfaction.

TOMATO WATER

This recipe should be made only in the summertime, when tomatoes are fresh and in season. That's when tomatoes will be the juiciest and yield the most water. Tomato Water can be used for a cold soup base, or served with any fish. It has a light, bright tomato flavor that's perfect for hot days.

YIELD: 6 TO 8 SERVINGS

3 lbs (1.4 kg) fresh tomatoes

2 red jalapeños

3 basil sprigs

1 tbsp (15 g) salt

1 tbsp (15 ml) rice wine vinegar

Puree all ingredients in a blender until smooth.

Line a fine mesh-sieve with a piece of cheese cloth and place it over a large bowl. Pour the tomato mixture into the sieve and allow it to sit in the refrigerator overnight.

The next day, squeeze out any remaining water from the tomato mixture. Discard the solids and keep the liquid. Store in an airtight container for up to 3 days in the refrigerator.

Note

If the Tomato Water is a bit cloudy, that's fine. If you don't want any cloudiness, then simply strain it through the cheese cloth once more.

LEMON BUTTERMILK PANNA COTTA WITH FRESH BLUEBERRIES

This dessert is perfect for summer: It's light, tangy and not too decadent. Blueberries thrive in the summertime so feel free to garnish the panna cotta with a few extra berries and whipped cream. Alternatively, you could cook down a pint (170 g) of blueberries with ½ cup (96 g) of sugar to make a blueberry sauce to go over the panna cotta.

YIELD: 6 SERVINGS

3 ¾ cups (887 ml) heavy cream

1 ¾ cups (335 g) sugar

1 ½ vanilla pods, split lengthwise

4 tsp (18 g) gelatin

4 ½ cups (1.1 l) buttermilk

3 lemons, zested and juiced

1 pint (170 g) blueberries

Pour the cream and sugar into a small saucepan. Scrape the seeds from the vanilla pod into the pan and add the entire pod. Heat over medium heat until the sugar is dissolved, about 3 to 5 minutes. Add the gelatin and stir to combine. Add the buttermilk, lemon zest and juice and stir. Strain the mixture into another bowl.

Divide the blueberries equally into six 8-ounce (230-g) ramekins. Slowly pour the strained custard over them. Refrigerate until set, about 4 hours.

To unmold, dip the ramekins into hot water and invert the panna cotta onto serving plates. Top with fresh blueberries.

CORN CHOWDER WITH MARINATED TOMATOES

This rich, creamy and somewhat sweet chowder is delicious, especially when made with seasonal butter or sugar corn. Any fresh corn will work in this recipe, but butter and sugar corn are my favorites.

YIELD: 6 TO 8 SERVINGS

2 cups (440 g) chopped bacon

6 cups (909 g) diced onions

2 cups (303 g) diced celery

6 cups (1.2 kg) shucked corn

8 tbsp (115 g) butter

1 ½ cups (187 g) flour

4 cups (946 ml) Corn Stock (page 199)

6 cups (1.4 l) heavy cream

2 tsp (10 g) Old Bay® seasoning

1 tbsp (15 g) salt

2 tsp (10 g) pepper

2 tbsp (5 g) chopped thyme

4 cups (804 g) small dice potatoes

3 tbsp (44 ml) Tabasco®

Marinated Tomatoes (page 176)

In a large rondeau, or wide and shallow pot, cook the bacon over medium heat until its fat is rendered out. Add the onions, celery and corn to the pan and cook for 10 minutes. Add the butter and flour and continue cooking for 10 more minutes. While stirring, add the stock and cream. Then add the Old Bay® seasoning, salt, pepper, thyme, potatoes and Tabasco®. Cook until the potatoes are tender, about 8 to 10 minutes. Garnish with the Marinated Tomatoes.

Once cooled, the chowder can be stored in an airtight container in the refrigerator for up to 3 days. If it's too thick when reheating it, just add a little bit of water or milk to reach your desired consistency.

Note

This recipe can easily be made gluten-free by omitting the flour. The chowder won't be as thick, but it'll still be delicious.

MARINATED TOMATOES

These tomatoes are a great garnish to any rich dish, such as the Corn Chowder (page 175)
or a fatty piece of grilled meat. The sweet tomatoes take on a pickled flavor once they're marinated,
and they have just the right amount of acidity to balance out decadent meals.
This recipe is best made with summer tomatoes that are at their prime.

YIELD: 6 SERVINGS

1 pint (551 g) cherry tomatoes, cut in half

2 tbsp (25 g) finely diced shallots

2 tbsp (5 g) basil chiffonade

¼ cup (59 ml) sherry vinegar

1 ½ cups (355 ml) olive oil

1 tbsp (15 g) salt

1 tsp pepper

Combine all ingredients and allow to marinate for 20 minutes before serving.

Store covered in the refrigerator for 2 to 3 days.

PEACHES AND CREAM SALAD

This salad is a fun interpretation of the classic summertime dessert. Although it's a salad, it's still creamy and slightly sweet, with a nice acidity from the Pickled Peaches.

YIELD: 4 SERVINGS

PICKLED PEACHES

2 ½ lbs (1.3 kg) peaches

1 ½ cups (355 ml) Champagne vinegar

1 vanilla bean, split

1 cup (201 g) brown sugar

2 tsp (6 g) pink peppercorns

2 cups (473 ml) water

1 tsp chili flakes

½ tsp cloves

2 tbsp (30 g) salt

2 ounces (55 g) fresh thyme sprigs

1 cup (121 g) crème fraîche

¼ cup (59 ml) pickling liquid from Pickled Peaches

6 sliced Pickled Peaches

2 cups (80 g) arugula

¼ cup (43 g) pistachios, toasted

1 tsp salt

To make the pickled peaches, cut the peaches in half and remove their pits. Slice peaches into ¼-inch (6-mm)- thick slices and set aside in a large bowl.

In a pot, bring the remaining ingredients to a boil over high heat. Once it reaches a boil, remove from heat and set aside. Cover the peach slices with just enough ice to cover them. Pour the boiled liquid over them, cover and refrigerate for 24 hours before using.

In a bowl, whisk the crème fraîche and pickling liquid together. Add the remaining ingredients and toss until thoroughly coated. Serve right away.

BUTTER POACHED LOBSTER ROLLS WITH LEMON AIOLI

Nothing says summertime in New England like lobster rolls! I love the combination of butter and citrus in this recipe; it's the perfect balance of lemon to brighten up an otherwise rich dish. I like serving these in brioche rolls, but feel free to use any type of bread you like. You can even omit the bread completely and serve the lobster as a salad. The combination of the warm, buttery lobster with the cold iceberg lettuce is a nice contrast.

YIELD: 4 SERVINGS

2 lobsters

4 tbsp (57 g) butter

1 tbsp (15 ml) lemon juice

1 tsp salt

1 tbsp (3 g) chopped parsley

1 cup (40 g) iceberg lettuce, chiffonade

3 tbsp (41 g) Lemon Aioli (page 183)

4 brioche rolls

Split each lobster by inserting a knife into its head. Remove the head, keeping the claws separate from the tails. Set the heads aside for the broth.

Bring a pot of water to a boil. Place the lobster tails in a large bowl, and place the lobster claws in a separate large bowl. Add enough boiling water to cover the tails and allow to sit for 6 minutes. Do the same with the claws and allow them to sit for 8 minutes. Remove the tails and claws from the water and crack their shells to release the meat. Removing the meat from its shell does take some practice, so don't worry if it's not the prettiest looking meat.

Cut the tail meat in half, then cube it. The claw meat can also be cut, but I usually leave whole for garnish.

Heat the butter in a sauté pan over medium-low heat and add the lobster meat. Gently warm the lobster and add the lemon juice, salt and parsley. Remove from heat and set aside.

Mix the iceberg lettuce and aioli to thoroughly dress the lettuce.

To assemble the rolls, place some lettuce on each brioche roll and add some of the lobster meat on top. Serve right away.

Note

The lobster should be served warm, otherwise the butter will coagulate and it won't be very appetizing.

LEMON AIOLI

This bright, lemony sauce complements seafood perfectly, especially the Butter Poached Lobster Rolls (page 180). Use it like you would mayonnaise, or to dip crispy roasted potatoes in.

YIELD: 6 TO 8 SERVINGS

1 ½ oz (43 g) garlic cloves
3 ½ oz (99 g) egg yolks
1 tbsp (16 g) Dijon mustard
1 cup (237 ml) lemon juice
½ cup (118 ml) olive oil
5 cups (1.2 l) canola oil
1 ½ tbsp (23 g) salt

Add the garlic, egg yolks, mustard and lemon juice to a food processor. Puree until the garlic is smooth. While the food processor is running, slowly drizzle in the olive and canola oils until emulsified. Season with salt.

Aioli will keep for up to a week if refrigerated in an airtight container.

GRILLED SALMON WITH PEPERONATA AND ZUCCHINI FRITTERS

This is a great summertime recipe for grilling with friends on a sunny day.
The tangy peppers and rich fritters work famously with the flavor of the salmon.
It's not too heavy or decadent—perfect for an outdoor meal.

YIELD: SERVES 4

4 (4-oz [113-g]) salmon steaks

1 tsp salt

1 tsp pepper

1 tbsp (15 ml) canola oil

1 cup (170 g) Peperonata (page 187)

1 recipe Zucchini Fritters (page 187)

Heat a grill, or grill pan, to medium-high heat.

Pat salmon steaks dry with a paper towel. Season with the salt and pepper, and rub the canola oil on it. Place steaks on the grill and allow to cook for 8 minutes, uninterrupted. Flip and cook for another 8 minutes, uninterrupted.

Remove salmon from grill and serve alongside the Peperonata and fritters.

Note

Feel free to use any kind of fish in this recipe—I just like the flavor combination of salmon, peppers and zucchini.

PEPERONATA

Peperonata is a spicy and tangy marinade of red and yellow peppers. It makes for a great condiment for many grilled items and it's great on sandwiches with leftover grilled meat.

YIELD: SERVES 6

2 lbs (907 g) red peppers

2 lbs (907 g) yellow peppers

2 tbsp (19 g) chopped garlic

¼ cup (50 g) diced shallots

1 jalapeño, diced

3 tbsp (8 g) thyme leaves

½ tbsp (2 g) chopped oregano

¼ cup (59 ml) Champagne vinegar

2 tbsp (30 g) salt

Char the peppers over an open flame until their skins are blackened. If you don't have access to an open flame, you can also grill them. Remove from the fire and place in a bowl. Cover and allow to steam for 15 minutes. Remove the skins by rubbing the peppers with a paper towel.

Julienne the peppers and place them in a large bowl. Add the remaining ingredients and mix until thoroughly combined. Allow to marinate overnight before using.

ZUCCHINI FRITTERS

These fritters are just like pancakes, except lighter and savory. They're a delicious appetizer or a great pairing to grilled meats. Make them in the summer, when zucchini is fresh and abundant.

YIELD: MAKES 10 TO 12 FRITTERS

2 ½ lbs (1 kg) zucchini

1 onion

4 tbsp (60 g) salt, divided

¼ cup (12 g) chopped scallions

1 tbsp (10 g) diced jalapeño

2 tsp (2 g) chopped dill

3 eggs

¼ cup (45 g) grated Parmesan cheese

2 cups (250 g) flour

4 tbsp (60 ml) canola oil

Using a box grater, grate the zucchini and onion. Season with 3 tablespoons (45 g) of salt. Allow to drain in a large chinois, or very fine mesh sieve, for 20 minutes.

Combine the scallions, jalapeño and dill with the eggs, Parmesan and flour in a medium bowl. Add the zucchini-onion mixture to the flour-egg mixture in batches and mix. Season with 1 tablespoon (15 g) of salt.

Heat 1 tablespoon (15 ml) of the canola oil in a large sauté pan over medium heat. Using a large ladle, add the zucchini batter to the pan and gently flatten it. If the batter is sticking to the ladle, you can grease it with extra oil. Cook the batter like a pancake, until it browns on one side, 3 to 4 minutes. Flip and cook the other side. Repeat with the remaining canola oil and batter. Transfer the fritters to a paper towel to drain.

PORK CHOPS WITH WATERMELON BBQ SAUCE AND PICKLED WATERMELON

There's nothing more summery than watermelon and BBQ, and this recipe combines both to create a light and fun dish. It's perfect for an afternoon of grilling with friends. I like to serve it with cold beer and cornbread, or even just plain grilled corn with spicy butter.

YIELD: SERVES 4

8 (7 to 8-oz [198- to 227-g]) pork chops

2 tbsp (30 g) salt

1 tbsp (15 g) pepper

4 cups (946 ml) Watermelon BBQ Sauce (page 191)

2 cups (360 g) Pickled Watermelon (page 191)

Heat grill, or a grill pan, on high heat.

Season pork chops with the salt and pepper. Grill on high heat for 10 to 12 minutes per side. Brush the pork chops with 2 tablespoons (15 g) of BBQ sauce and grill for another 4 minutes on each side. Pork chops are done when they reach 145°F (63°C). Remove from heat and brush with however much BBQ sauce you like. Garnish with Pickled Watermelon and serve right away.

WATERMELON BBQ SAUCE

This BBQ sauce is the epitome of summer. It also happens to be very versatile.
I like to pair it with grilled pork, but it works well with chicken or fish, too.
It does take some time to make, but the end result is worth it.

YIELD: 8 CUPS (1.9 ML)

1 watermelon

1 lb (454 g) Spanish onions, sliced

½ lb (227 g) red onions, sliced

3 tbsp (44 ml) canola oil

½ cup (78 g) chopped garlic

2 jalapeños, sliced

1 tbsp (8 g) ground cumin

4 cups (644 g) canned tomatoes

1 cup (237 ml) molasses

2 ½ cups (592 ml) cider vinegar

½ cup (118 ml) lime juice

2 tbsp (30 g) salt

Wash and dry the watermelon. Remove the skin and set aside for pickling.

In a large stockpot over medium heat, sauté the onions with the canola oil until they caramelize, about 10 minutes. Add the garlic and jalapeño and cook until they soften, about 5 minutes. Add the cumin and tomatoes and cook until most of the liquid is gone, about 15 minutes. Add the molasses and vinegar and cook for 20 minutes. Puree the fresh watermelon in a blender, then add to the stockpot mixture and cook for another 20 minutes. Remove from heat. Add the lime juice and salt. Puree mixture using an immersion blender, or in batches if using a regular blender.

PICKLED WATERMELON

This is a resourceful and delicious way to use up the watermelon rinds you'll have left over from making Watermelon BBQ Sauce. When pickled, watermelon rinds take on a cucumber pickle texture with a sweet and tangy flavor.

YIELD: 12 TO 14 SERVINGS

1 watermelon, rinds only

¼ cup (33 g) sliced shallots

2 tbsp (19 g) sliced garlic

1 cup (192 g) sugar

1 tsp ground cumin

1 tsp ground coriander

1 ½ tsp (1 g) red pepper flakes

1 tsp celery seeds

1 ½ tsp (5 g) mustard seeds

5 bay leaves

3 ½ cups (828 ml) cider vinegar

3 cups (710 ml) water

2 tbsp (30 g) salt

Julienne the watermelon rinds. Set aside.

Add the remaining ingredients in a saucepan and bring to a boil. Remove from the heat and allow to cool to room temperature. Pour over the watermelon rinds and allow to pickle for 24 hours in the refrigerator before using.

GRILLED PINEAPPLE WITH COCONUT ZABAGLIONE AND COCONUT BISCOTTI

This dish can be served either warm right off the grill or at room temperature.
I love the hint of smokiness and caramel flavor that the pineapple develops from being grilled.
Zabaglione is a light and airy Italian custard. The classic combination of coconut and lime
in this recipe makes it an ideal summer dessert.

YIELD: SERVES 8

1 pineapple, with the skin removed and cut into 1 ½-inch (38-mm) thick pieces

2 tbsp (30 g) salt

2 tsp (5 g) ground cinnamon

COCONUT ZABAGLIONE

2 ¾ cups (651 ml) coconut milk

2 limes, zested

½ vanilla bean

3 tbsp (45 ml) honey

6 egg yolks

¼ cup (59 ml) rum

1 cup (237 ml) heavy cream

Coconut Biscotti (page 195)

Heat grill, or grill pan, on high heat. Season the pineapple pieces with salt and cinnamon. Grill pineapple until they're soft and have grill marks, about 4 to 6 minutes. Set aside.

To make the zabaglione, add the coconut milk and lime zest to a heavy-bottomed saucepan. Cut the vanilla bean in half lengthwise and scrape out its seeds into the saucepan. Cook on low heat, keeping the liquid just below a simmer. When it's reduced to about ¼ cup (59 ml), add the honey and reduce until syrupy, about 10 to 12 minutes. Stir frequently to prevent it from burning. Set syrup aside.

Add the egg yolks to a double boiler and slowly whisk in the coconut syrup and rum. Keep whisking until the mixture is creamy, fluffy and frothy. Make sure not to overheat the egg yolks or they'll cook too quickly and form lumps. When the mixture has thickened, 4 to 5 minutes, remove from heat and continue whisking to cool. Set aside to cool completely.

Using a mixer with the whisk attachment, whip the heavy cream to soft peaks. Fold the whipped cream into the egg yolk mixture until incorporated. Serve right away, with the grilled pineapple and biscotti.

COCONUT BISCOTTI

Biscotti may seem overwhelming the first time you make it, but it's actually quite easy once you get the hang of it. This recipe is like your traditional biscotti, but with a lightly sweet coconut taste that's absolutely delicious with Coconut Zabaglione (page 192) and Grilled Pineapple (page 192). It's also great for dunking into your afternoon coffee or tea.

YIELD: MAKES 10 TO 12 BISCOTTI

1 ½ cups (187 g) flour, plus more for flouring your rolling surface

¾ tsp baking powder

¼ tsp baking soda

¼ tsp salt

⅛ tsp nutmeg

¾ cup (144 g) sugar

1 tsp vanilla

2 large eggs

1 cup (76 g) sweetened coconut flakes, toasted until golden

Preheat the oven to 300°F (149°C).

In a medium bowl, combine the flour, baking powder, baking soda, salt and nutmeg. Set aside.

Add the sugar, vanilla and eggs to the bowl of a KitchenAid® mixer with the paddle attachment. Beat for 2 minutes on medium-high speed until thick. Add the dry ingredients and mix just until combined. Stir in the coconut flakes.

Turn the dough out onto a floured surface. Knead 7 to 8 times. Shape the dough into a 15 x 3 inch (38 x 7.6 cm) log. Place on a parchment-lined cookie sheet and pat to a 1 inch (2.5 cm) thickness.

Bake in the preheated oven until golden brown, about 40 minutes. Cool for 5 minutes on a wire rack.

Once cool enough to handle, cut diagonally into 1 inch (2.5 cm) slices and return to the cookie sheet. Bake for 20 minutes, or until thoroughly toasted. Remove from cookie sheet and cool on a wire rack.

Store covered at room temperature for up to 3 days.

Serve with Grilled Pineapple (page 192) and Coconut Zabaglione (page 192).

Stocks

CHICKEN STOCK

Good homemade stock is always great to have around.
It's significantly better than the store-bought stuff. I always freeze extra stock
in ice trays for later use. They'll last for up to 2 months in the freezer if covered.

YIELD: 8 CUPS [1.9 L]

5 lbs (2.3 kg) chicken bones

2 tbsp (30 ml) canola oil

2 onions, sliced

4 carrots, peeled and roughly chopped

Water

Preheat the oven to 400°F (205°C).

Place the chicken bones on a cookie sheet and roast until browned, about 45 minutes.

Add the canola oil to a stockpot over high heat. Sweat the onions and carrots for 5 minutes. Add the roasted chicken bones and add enough cold water to completely cover. Bring to a simmer and cook for 3 hours.

Strain, discarding any solids, and cool.

VEGETABLE STOCK

YIELD: 12 CUPS [2.8 L]

2 tbsp (30 g) canola oil

2 onions, sliced

5 carrots, peeled and roughly chopped

1 bunch of celery, roughly chopped

2 green apples, cored and cut into chunks

3 bay leaves

2 tbsp (17 g) peppercorns

1 oz (28 g) thyme

2 oz (57 g) parsley

Water

Heat a large stock pot over high heat and pour in all of the ingredients, adding enough cold water to cover everything. Simmer for 1 ½ hours. Strain, discarding any solids, and cool.

MUSHROOM STOCK

Mushroom stock is a great option to have when cooking vegetarian meals.
Use it in any recipe where you would use a meat stock.

YIELD: 8 TO 10 CUPS (1.9 TO 2.4 L)

1 tbsp (15 ml) canola oil

2 onions, sliced

2 lbs (907 g) whole mushrooms or mushroom stems

1 cup (237 ml) sherry wine

2 oz (57 g) thyme sprigs

1 tbsp (9 g) peppercorns

Water

Heat a large stockpot over high heat. Add the canola oil and onions. Cook until they begin to caramelize, about 8 minutes. Add the mushrooms and sherry wine and cook until most of the wine is reduced. Add the thyme, peppercorns and enough cold water to completely cover all ingredients. Simmer for 1 hour. Strain, discarding of any solids, and allow to cool.

Fill ice cube trays with stock and freeze for up to 2 months.

CORN STOCK

I'm always trying to find ways to waste as little food as possible,
and this recipe is a great way to do just that. When you find yourself with leftover corn cobs,
this stock makes great use of them. This delicate stock is perfect for the Corn Chowder (page 175)
recipe, or to simply add a light corn flavor in whatever dish you choose.

YIELD: 12 CUPS (2.8 L)

1 onion, sliced

4 leeks, sliced

6 corn cobs

¼ oz (10 g) thyme sprigs

2 bay leaves

2 tbsp (17 g) peppercorns

Water, enough to cover all ingredients

In a stock pot over medium heat, sweat out the onions and leeks for 6 minutes. Add the remaining ingredients and bring to a simmer for 2 hours. Strain the stock, discarding the solids, and chill immediately.

Refrigerated stock will keep for up to 4 days, while frozen stock will stay fresh for 2 months.

ABOUT THE AUTHOR

STACY COGSWELL was born in Quincy, Massachusetts, and grew up in a small town called Wareham, on the border of Cape Cod. She graduated from Johnson & Wales University in 2005 with a degree in culinary arts. Shortly after graduation, Stacy moved to Boston and worked in several well-known restaurants with highly talented chefs, who taught her what it means to cook professionally. She's traveled to Europe, Southeast Asia and the Caribbean, learning about foods in different cultures around the globe. In 2014, Stacy was a contestant on Bravo's *Top Chef: Boston*. Stacy currently resides in Boston with her fiancé and works at Liquid Art House restaurant.

ACKNOWLEDGMENTS

Thank you to the Bouchard and Cogswell family for being the most supportive family anyone could ever ask for.

Thank you to my extremely supportive fiancé, Robert Deetz, who has been very patient throughout this entire process.

Thank you to the Page Street Publishing team for giving me this opportunity.

Thank you to Taissa Rebroff for all her assistance in making this book happen.

Thank you to everyone I've met throughout my career. You've helped mold me into the chef I am today.

Finally, thank *you*, for reading these words and cooking these recipes.

INDEX